/250

W9-BKA-591

883

A HISTORY OF DESIGN FROM THE VICTORIAN ERA TO THE PRESENT

**A survey of the Modern style
in architecture, interior design,
industrial design, graphic design,
and photography**

ANN FEREBEE

Henry Alken. The Progress of Steam,
England. 1828

VNR VAN NOSTRAND REINHOLD COMPANY
——————————————— New York

First published in paperback in 1980
Copyright © 1970 by Van Nostrand Reinhold Company Inc.
Library of Congress Catalog Card Number 68-16033
ISBN 0-442-23115-6

Van Nostrand Reinhold Company Inc.
135 West 50th Street, New York, NY 10020

Van Nostrand Reinhold Australia Pty. Ltd.
480 La Trobe Street, Melbourne, Victoria 3000

Van Nostrand Reinhold Company Ltd.
Molly Millars Lane, Wokingham, Berkshire, England RG11 2PY

Macmillan of Canada
Division of Gage Publishing Ltd.
164 Commander Boulevard
Agincourt, Ont., M1S 3C7

16 15 14 13 12 11 10 9 8 7

PREFACE

Modern Design: Fingerprint of a Culture

This book presents a visual record of the artifacts of the first industrial society. With the introduction of new energy sources, satellite communication and computer controlled information networks, we are now embarking on a second industrial age and the articulation of a new esthetic. Punctuated by these developments and by the death of its great form-givers—Corbusier, Mies and Wright—Modern design, as we have known it for more than a century, slips into the past.

It seems evident that the designers of the emerging culture, or, as today's students call it, the Counter Culture, will be less concerned with objects *per se* and more concerned with process (user involvement, industrialization of housing, systems (transportation, communication) and values (needs of the poor, preservation of nature and of the best of our man-made environment). These designers will question the practitioners of Modern design for glorifying technology while neither recognizing its harmful effect nor using it to produce low-cost but well-designed goods for mass consumption. In addition to presenting much that has not been systematically catalogued before, a main purpose of the present survey is to help provide a framework for a more responsible design esthetic.

CONTENTS

Lewis W. Hine. *Man at Dynamo.* c. 1921

Staff design. "Turnip" watch,
Hamilton Watch Co, USA. 1892–1925

Thomas Adams. Clock "in Gothic fashion,"
England. 1851

John Bell. Hours clock, England. 1851

INTRODUCTION

The three timepieces at left may be seen as examples of three conventionally accepted styles: Victorian, Art Nouveau, and Modern. The two clocks, though so different from each other, were designed in the same year in the same city. How can two such differing styles exist side by side? What is meant by style, anyway, and why is it important? Style is the designer's language. Its grammar consists of form, line, color, texture, and material. In coherently combining these elements, designers make statements—statements that are important because they provide a key to understanding the culture from which they emerge.

The statement made by the designer of the Hamilton watch is quite different from those made a generation earlier by the designers of the two clocks. That he is concerned with function where they had been concerned with ornament is obvious from the emphasis on the legibility of the watchface and the reduction of the silhouette to a simple circle. The Hamilton watch looks like the efficient precision instrument that it was. The Hours clock and the Gothic clock, though they may have worked equally well, look like household ornaments. The designer's emphasis—on function or on ornament—is one factor in determining his style. Equally important are the messages expressed through particular forms and ornamental idioms. What makes the Hamilton watch Modern is not simply the designer's concern with function to the exclusion of ornament. It is also his decision to work with geometric forms derived from the world of machines rather than the biomorphic forms of nature.

The method of production also affects style. An important distinction between the Hamilton watch and the two clocks, for example, is that the watch was made by means of a steam-powered system of factory production, while the clocks were made by hand. The history of the industrial age of design and the new forms that derived from industrial technology begins roughly with the crowning of Queen Victoria in 1837. By that date the McCormick reaper (page 33), sans serif type (page 42) and other artifacts incorporating the new geometric and straight-lined forms had already appeared.

How did the new factory system, enhanced by the development of the Corless steam engine, modify design? It broke the work process into separate fragments, displacing handcraft techniques that had not altered for a thousand years. No longer did a single master control production from drawing board to finished product. The numbers of skilled workers practicing handcraft became fewer as they found themselves unable to match the cost of factory products. Many handcrafted articles disappeared from the marketplace. And the new tastemakers, the factory owners, began to produce products whose design was dictated by the efficient use of the new technology.

The design arts were affected also by the transformation which the factory system wrought on the quality of life and on the environment. Karl Marx summed up the social and cultural importance of production modes: "The hand-mill gives you society with the feudal lord; the steam-mill, society with the industrial capitalist. A certain mode of production, or industrial stage, is always combined with a certain mode of cooperation, or social stage, and men, in changing their mode of production, change their way of living and change all their social relations." Marx was right. The new factory technology transformed England and America and, more slowly, Europe, from agrarian to industrial economies. It transformed the farmer into a factory worker and converted the countryside into teeming cities.

The new technology challenged the imagination of progressive architects and other designers. A radically different, machine-produced, machine-inspired style was predicated on a new esthetic of function. At the same time, the new technology fomented a regression to styles of the past by threatening the social, ethical, and esthetic values of most designers.

Victorian painters also found themselves in two camps: one welcomed the new technological environment, the other concentrated on the natural landscape. Albert Bierstaedt, leading painter of the Hudson River School, depicts in *Yosemite Valley* (overleaf) an American Eden, not the squalid factories of New England's textile towns. Other artists found technology an exciting subject. Turner's *Rain, Steam and Speed* (overleaf) shrouds the locomotive in glamorous clouds of steam. George Innes, in his more prosaic presentation of the railway, indicates acceptance if not enthusiasm for the iron horse.

The Dynamo and the Virgin

The American historian Henry Adams was deeply affected by the new technology. In *The Education of Henry Adams,* he reports his reaction to the great hall of dynamos at the 1900 Paris Exposition. To him a dynamo was more than an ingenious channel for converting coal into electricity. He began to think of it as a mysterious but palpable moral force, much as the early Christians had thought of the Virgin. "She was the animated dynamo; she was reproduction —the greatest and most mysterious of all energies . . . All the steam in the world," Adams wrote, "could not, like the Virgin, build Chartres." To Adams the Dynamo and the Virgin symbolized all the conflicting forces in modern life: machine and nature, production and reproduction, power and love, utility and beauty, science and religion, present and past.

Victorian sensibility was thus polarized into a feeling for nature and against technology, on the one hand, and for technology and away from nature on

Anthony Walker. *Prior Park,* earliest view of an English railway. 1752

Corless engine. Philadelphia Centennial, USA. 1876

Anonymous. *Dowlas from the Cinder Heaps, Illustrated London News,* Feb. 13, 1875

Albert Bierstaedt. *Yosemite Valley*, USA. 1866

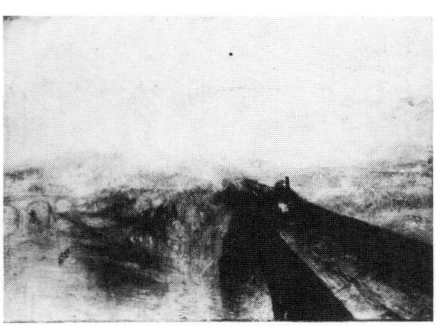

J. M. Turner. *Rain, Steam and Speed*, England. 1844.

George Inness. *The Lackawanna Valley*, USA. 1855

the other. From the Victorian period until the present design style has remained polarized into machine-oriented and nature-oriented modes. However, we have become accustomed to equating the historical terms "Victorian," "Art Nouveau," and "Modern" with different styles in design and ignoring the importance of these two modes as fundamental elements of style. A more useful way of looking at design during the industrial age is to trace the expression of the machine-oriented and nature-oriented modes through their early (Victorian), middle (Art Nouveau) and late (Modern or 20th Century) developmental stages. In each stage, building and objects expressing either mode will be found to share a set of characteristics.

Machine-affirming artifacts tend toward geometric form and angular line, and are made by machine-based techniques utilizing glass, steel, concrete and other industrial materials. Hard and smooth-surfaced, they are often painted from a primary palette of red, yellow or blue. For ease of reference and to reflect the refinements which appeared in each stage, such machine-affirming artifacts will be designated proto-Functionalist during the Victorian period, Rectilinear during the Art Nouveau interval and Functionalist in the 20th Century.

Artifacts affirming the nature-oriented mode tend toward biomorphic forms, curved lines and wood, stone and other natural materials. Such materials lend themselves to hand-based fabrication techniques and result in artifacts that are usually rough-textured. Russet, brown, green and other nature-related shades predominate. Artifacts sharing these characteristics will be designated Picturesque in the Victorian period, as Curvilinear in the Art Nouveau interval and as Expressionist in the 20th Century or Modern period.

The three charts shown here diagram the stylistic elements of each mode during each period or stage of development, from the time of Victoria to the present.

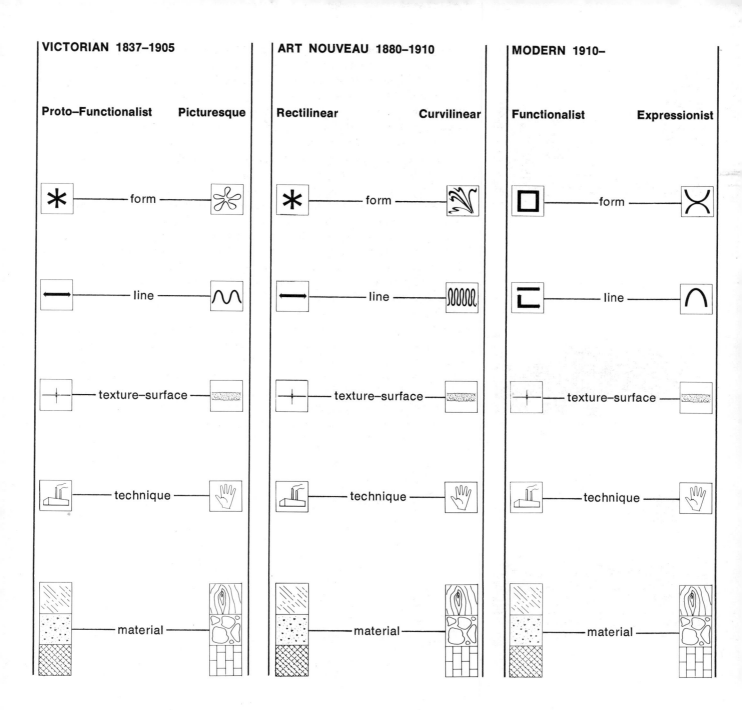

VICTORIAN DESIGN

**The Industrial Revolution
Precipitates a Crisis in Style**

Joseph Paxton. Crystal Palace, London. 1851

VICTORIAN ARCHITECTURE

Victorian architecture illustrates the manner in which style, in the middle of the 19th century, divided into a Picturesque mode and a proto-Functionalist mode. The Crystal Palace, which was the home of London's Great Exposition of 1851, exemplifies the proto-Functionalist mode. When Joseph Paxton (1801–1865), the brilliant landscape gardener, undertook the design of the Crystal Palace he discarded all architectural preconceptions. He selected industrial materials and devised a new fabrication system, both of which dominated and were inseparable from the building style.

Paxton adapted the idea for the Crystal Palace from the greenhouses he had constructed for the Duke of Devonshire. Confident from previous experience in building glass houses, he specified an unprecedented 1,073,760 square feet of glass for the Crystal Palace. To speed up the work of installing the panes, Paxton made a track in the iron girders that framed the planned structure. Trolleys swiftly conveyed the glaziers up and down the tracks as they installed pane after pane.

Iron, the other material used in the construction of the Crystal Palace, was not new as a building material, but prefabricating was. By using it Paxton produced an unprecedented 6,024 wrought iron columns, 1,245 iron girders and 45 miles of standard-length sash bars. Prefabrication sped construction time, and limited on-site labor to mere assembly of ready-made parts. By reducing construction time, Paxton reduced costs. He completed the structure in February 1851, a miraculous seven months after the building committee had picked his plan over 245 others. At 800,000 square feet, the Crystal Palace was the largest single building the world had seen.

The Crystal Palace appeared to most Victorians to be "styleless"—at least it lacked the Greek columns and Gothic arches they associated with style. What they did not recognize was that its geometric form, its machine-like repetition of modules, its hard, glittering glass walls combined to make this Cathedral of Commerce the first major building to incorporate the proto-Functionalist mode. Its proto-Functionalism grew out of the way glass and iron parts had been factory-fabricated. Prefabrication, iron and glass—and Paxton, himself—foreshadowed three major design developments of the coming century: the machine as the molder of style, technology as the source of new building materials and the nonarchitect as architectural innovator. More than that, as the prototype of the steel-ribbed glass cage, the Crystal Palace introduced the most compelling preoccupation in modern architectural design. This preoccupation would be reflected in dozens of replications over the next century, until, with the Seagram building, the sylistic problems of the glass cage would be ultimately resolved.

Joseph Paxton. Crystal Palace, prefabricated parts, London. 1851

Joseph Paxton. Crystal Palace, oak tree, London. 1851

14

The Rise of the Picturesque

The Crystal Palace was an anomaly. By 1851, the rest of English Victorian architecture had fallen under the sway of the Gothic Revival, the most popular expression of the Picturesque mode. The Middle Ages were recreated in the Houses of Parliament. Designed by Sir Charles Barry (1830–1880), these irregularly silhouetted buildings introduced neo-Gothic architecture in public buildings and inflamed an already avid taste for the Picturesque.

Barry and his contemporaries adorned facades with Gothic trefoils to evoke longing for the past. At home with keyhole arches from Spain and minarets from the Near East, architects sought, through such devices, to arouse a yearning for exotic places. Dismayed by the clock-run industrial world they had helped invent, Victorian architects must have felt that any time, any place was better than their own.

Sir Charles Barry. Houses of Parliament, London. 1837–1857

A. W. N. Pugin (1812–1852), a gifted draftsman with an unrivaled knowledge of Gothic decoration, led the Gothic Revival in England. The architectural details which Pugin designed for the Houses of Parliament gave him popularity. His conversion to Catholicism intensified Pugin's interest in England's Gothic churches, which had originally been Catholic. And the more he associated the Roman Catholic faith with Gothic architecture, the more he dedicated himself to spreading neo-Gothic architecture throughout England. Feverishly active, Pugin designed, decorated or restored more than 35 churches. His witty *True Principles of Pointed or Christian Architecture* failed to convert England to Catholicism, but it did kindle enthusiasm for neo-Gothic architecture.

A.W.N. Pugin. House of Lords, interior, London. 1840

The Albert Memorial of Sir George Gilbert Scott (1811–1878) epitomized the Gothic Revival. A 175-foot spire dwarfs the figure of Prince Albert. Over-rich ornament obscures basic structure, and polychromatic marble completes an effect that is more grandiose than grand.

The Gothic Revival was only one aspect of what turned out to be a century-long battle not only between the proto-Functionalist and Picturesque modes, but among various expressions of the Picturesque mode. Neo-Moorish, neo-Turkish and neo-Egyptian styles evoked sensual, erotic associations just as neo-Gothic had evoked the spiritual and the religious. John Nash's Brighton Pavilion had delighted Regency fairgoers with its whiff of the seraglio. Owen Jones (1809–1874), an influential writer as well as designer, further promoted what may be called the Levantine Revival, an adaptation of motifs from the architecture of Turkey, Egypt, and other Levantine countries. Jones's *Plans, Elevations, Sections and Details of the Alhambra* (1836) introduced neo-Moorish architecture to England and encouraged the taste for the exotic. His Alhambra and Egyptian courts, exhibited at the Crystal Palace, did for neo-Levantine styles what Pugin's Gothic court had done for neo-Gothic. Jones's

Sir George Gilbert Scott. Albert Memorial, London. 1864–1872

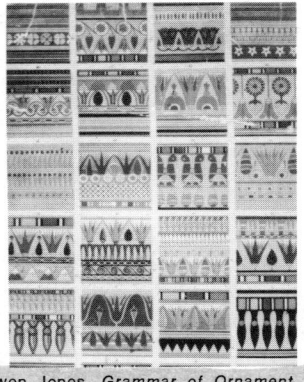

Owen Jones. *Grammar of Ornament,* Egyptian decorative motifs, England. 1868

Charles Garnier. Paris Opéra, Paris. 1861

Charles Garnier. Paris Opéra, interior, Paris. 1861

most ambitious book, *Grammar of Ornament* (1856), contains 3,000 color plates splendidly explicating the decorative details of Greek, Roman and Gothic as well as Egyptian, Persian and other Levantine styles. These superb plates influenced designers of English wallpaper, fabric and furniture for nearly half a century and made Jones England's most influential interior designer—until the advent of William Morris.

Although the Gothic expression of the Picturesque mode was more popular than the neo-Levantine and neo-classic, the varieties of each grew increasingly numerous and confused. Yet the brooding neo-Gothic mansion was no more truly Gothic than today's ranch-type house is a working ranch. Neo-Gothic and neo-Egyptian were Picturesque adaptations, not resurrections of an original style. Each adaptation invariably revealed, by the insensitivity with which motifs were copied or by the inappropriateness of materials, that it was not what it pretended to be but only a Picturesque imitation.

Thus the effect of the Industrial Revolution on English architecture was twofold. It generated the first examples of buildings done in the proto-Functionalist mode. And it fomented such a strong regression to styles of the past, threatening the values of the majority of designers, that historicism became the most significant element in the Picturesque mode.

The esthetic of the Picturesque armed Victorian designers with aims and principles entirely different from those of proto-Functionalism. The term "Picturesque" first appeared in 17th-century Italy, but the English writer Uvedale Price wrote an *Essay on the Picturesque* (1884) that popularized the term as signifying design which utilized the technique of suggesting rather than stating. A visual analogue to the term "poetic," it introduced the idea that design could and did evoke feelings; that a Neo-Gothic church would evoke the spiritual and a neo-Levantine summer house the erotic. From this idea, it was a short step to the establishment of a Victorian esthetic under which many Victorian design critics judged, and many Victorian designers designed, in terms of moral relevance.

Iron and the French Engineers

Neo-Baroque rather than Gothic motifs dominated French architecture. The Paris Opera House, with garlands, busts and gilded masks, appealed more to the French taste for elaborate ornamentation than did the few stark proto-Functionalist designs of the period in France. Nevertheless, the proto-Functionalist designs predicted 20th-century architecture's main direction. Just as England's most significant example of proto-Functionalist architecture had been produced by a man unencumbered by classical architectural training, so

France's main proto-Functionalist structures were produced by engineers rather than architects. Henri Labrouste (1801–1875), for example, was trained as an engineer as well as an architect. This was important because 19th-century French architecture had become a highly specialized and academically narrow profession. Aligned with the art rather than the engineering schools, French architectural faculties failed to provide students with the technical training necessary for the utilization of the burgeoning building technology of the 19th century. Labrouste was among the few to prepare himself for it by taking degrees at the Ecole Polytechnique as well as the École des Beaux Arts. It was the technical training that gave Labrouste a superb grasp of the most advanced 19th-century building materials and a mastery of cast-iron construction.

Henri Labrouste. Bibliothèque Nationale, Paris. 1851

Although prehistoric men had fashioned tools from iron as early as 1200 B.C., neither Ancient nor Renaissance architects used it because until the 19th century it could not be smelted and forged in sufficient quantity. Labrouste was the first to use cast, as well as wrought, iron in an important building, the Bibliothèque Sainte-Genevieve. Although Labrouste concealed the wrought iron framework behind a neo-Renaissance exterior, the iron columns inside were open to public view.

Labrouste's masterpiece was another library, the Bibliothèque Nationale. To provide enough space for the library's 1,500,000-volume collection, Labrouste separated the stacks from the reading rooms—a new idea at the time. In the reading room he placed 16 iron columns to support spherical vaults. Each vault opened at the top to provide light for all desks. Beyond the reading room, the stacks extended four stories above ground and one story below ground. To provide light, Labrouste installed a cast-iron floor that allowed light to penetrate from the glass roof all the way down to the floor that was below ground. Such grid-floorplates, probably first used in the engine room of steamships, were so sensible that libraries still use them today.

Henri Labrouste. Bibliothèque Nationale, stacks, Paris. 1858

Gustave Eiffel (1832–1923), France's other pioneer of the proto-Functionalist mode, had also received initial training as an engineer. Before designing the cast-iron dirigible mast known as the Tour Eiffel for the Exposition of 1889, he had built a cast-iron bridge at Garabit, France, the locks for de Lesseps's ill-fated canal in Panama and the elegant iron skeleton for Bartholdi's Statue of Liberty in New York. While the public had admired Paxton's iron-and-glass box at London's Great Exposition, they were outraged when Eiffel's iron hat-pin began to rise—taller than the tallest building in the world—in the middle of Paris. Garnier petitioned the government to demolish the tower. The poet Paul Verlaine swore never to visit the Place d'Etoile again, while the English designer William Morris insisted on staying as near to its base as possible—in order to avoid seeing it. Amidst the uproar, only Thomas Edison recognized the structure for what it was: a prototype of the American skyscraper skeletons.

Gustave Eiffel. Eiffel Tower, Paris. 1887

A. J. Davis. Lyndhurst, Tarrytown, N.Y. 1838–1895

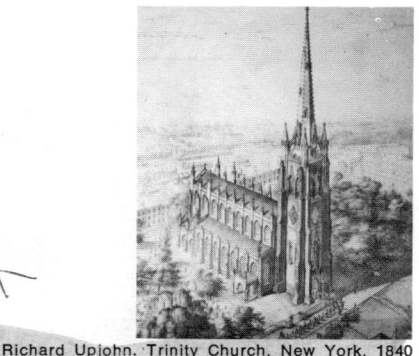

Richard Upjohn. Trinity Church, New York. 1840

James Renwick. Smithsonian Institution, Washington, D.C. 1846–1855

Eiffel, like Paxton, handled iron in a modern manner. He prefabricated 7,000 tons of girders, even prepunching the holes for rivets. A crew of only 250, all unskilled workers, erected the 1,000-foot-high tower. Eiffel anticipated the principle of reinforced concrete by making the wrought-iron bars that fastened the skeleton to its stone foundation serve also as reinforcement. Gate receipts from sightseers the first year proved Eiffel's case against his critics.

American Gothic

American architects, like those in England and Europe, responded in one of two ways to the Industrial Revolution. Either they rejected it by utilizing Picturesque revivalist forms or, like James Bogardus and a few others, they utilized industrial technology to devise new construction systems and explore the proto-Functionalist mode.

Picturesque forms began to appear in America after 1800, with the great neo-Greek Southern plantation houses. They persisted far into the 20th century in the neo-Gothic of New York's Church of St. John the Divine, of Pittsburgh's Cathedral of Learning and of other churches and schools seeking appropriately spiritual façades. By 1840 the architect Alexander Jackson Davis (1803–1892) and the New York tastemaker Andrew Jackson Downing had assured the public preference for neo-Gothic to neo-Greek. Downing commissioned Davis to make sketches of neo-Gothic cottages for publication in his popular books. A Hudson River Pugin, Davis then persuaded wealthy patrons to build their Hudson River retreats in the style that came to be called Hudson River Gothic. Lyndhurst, Jay Gould's country home and a key example of Picturesque in the United States, might have been modeled on the "Haunted Palace" in Poe's *House of Usher.* Its crenelated, gray-white Sing-Sing marble tower soars above other elements to produce a lofty, dramatic effect. The contradiction between the regularity of the floor plan and the irregularity of the façade reflects the conflict between the classic ideal of symmetry and the Romantic ideal of asymmetry. The turrets, trefoils, arches and other neo-Gothic architectural details express Victorian nostalgia for the idealism of the Medieval era. But, in the manner characteristic of the Picturesque mode, Lyndhurst betrays the artificiality of this sentiment. If the turrets and trefoils are pseudo-Gothic, then the idealism they express is pseudo-idealistic. This artificiality, reiterated in the interior, where canvas walls have been painted to imitate stone, echoes the hypocrisy sometimes associated with the Victorian temperament.

Two years after construction began on the Houses of Parliament, an English immigrant named Richard Upjohn (1828–1903) began work on New York's carefully proportioned Trinity Church. That church, together with the more massive Saint Patrick's Cathedral of James Renwick (1818–1895), popularized the neo-Gothic style for American churches. By 1855, Renwick's red-brick-towered Smithsonian Institution had sanctioned Picturesque for the nation's government buildings.

The Near Eastern ornament that designers had woven into English architecture also festooned 19th-century American buildings. Frederick Church, the last important member of the Hudson River School of Artists, built Olana (Arabic for "Castle on the Hill") in an amalgam of pseudo-Moorish and Italian styles. He decorated the interior with Persian brass and tiles, Moroccan pistols, Oriental bronzes, Turkish rugs, and doors stenciled with Arabic designs.

Architect Minard Lafever, although remembered mainly for his Greek-Revival town houses in Brooklyn Heights, designed the Old Whalers' Church in neo-Egyptian; John Haviland, whose specialty was prisons, designed New York's famous jail, The Tombs, to resemble an Egyptian temple. Toward the end of the century the Jewish community in New York began to acquire stability and wealth and built Park East, Central and other synagogues that borrowed elements of the Moorish style. The new synagogues summoned up the Sephardic culture of 15th-century Spain when Jewish learning experienced a great renaissance. The architects of the new synagogues relied on the Moorish keyhole arch and thus avoided the Christian connotations of the neo-Gothic pointed arch. Ironically, the keyhole arch, as one fundamental element in the mosques of the Muslim faith, carried its own set of religious connotations.

Henry Hobson Richardson (1838–1886), the most outstanding American architect in the half century before 1900, introduced the first native American style of domestic architecture at Newport, Rhode Island. Called shingle style, it reiterated a taste for the straightforward that began in the colonial days. In contrast to the imitation French chateaux and Italian villas that were soon to rise less than a mile from its site, the Watts Sherman house, with its exterior of brown wood shingles, blended with the oat grass and long leaf pine of Newport's sand-swept shore. A Richardson protegé, Stanford White (1853–1906), designed the now-destroyed Lowe House (page 21), possibly the finest shingle-style house of all. So popular did shingle summer-houses become that by 1910 they had darkened the seashore from Nags Head, North Carolina, to Blue Hill, Maine, to become enduring reminders of the "brown decades" in America.

The rest of Richardson's work lacked the purity, though not the power, of his shingle-style houses. Influenced by a Beaux Arts education, Richardson introduced Romanesque elements in his public buildings. So powerful was the effect of his public work that it generated a Romanesque revival whose influence on American homes, churches and office buildings would be seen for more than a generation. Richardson's Trinity Church in Boston (page 20), for which John LaFarge, William Morris, and Edward Burne-Jones designed

Frederick Church. Olana, Hudson, N.Y. 1870–1872

Minard Lafever. Old Whalers' Church, Sag Harbor, New York. 1844

Schneider and Herder. Park East Synagogue, New York. 1888–1890

Henry Hobson Richardson. Watts Sherman House, Newport, R.I. 1874–1876

Henry Hobson Richardson. Trinity Church, Boston. 1873–1877

Henry Hobson Richardson. Marshall Field Warehouse, Chicago. 1885–1887

stained-glass windows, epitomizes Richardson's neo-Romanesque style. Constructed of red Milford granite and dominated by a massive round-turreted central tower, it radiates masculine strength.

Having established his reputation with Trinity Church, Richardson turned to the seemingly prosaic task of creating a suitable design for a warehouse. Until the 19th century, architects thought of little but churches and palaces. But, with the Industrial Revolution, designs for warehouses for manufactured goods, factories, railway stations, department stores and office buildings began to challenge architects. Richardson determined not to conceal the prosaic function of the Marshall Field warehouse behind a highly decorative facade. Instead, he chose to rely on the great round-arched windows and the vigorous texture of red Missouri granite to provide interest. Perfect proportion and a perfect interrelationship of the seven stories to one another accounted for the excellence of his design. As the last important architect of the pre-steel age, Richardson influenced Louis Sullivan and, ultimately, Frank Lloyd Wright. The marks of his style—heavy wrought stone, rounded arch entrances and massive towers—persisted long after his death.

The railroad, mining and utilities magnates who rose to fortune after the Civil War turned to the Renaissance settings of the Medici rather than to the Gothic settings of the church to advertise their newly won status. The architect who most flamboyantly counterfeited the palaces they wanted was Richard Morris Hunt (1827–1895). Hunt's buildings, though not the equal of Richardson's, were glamorous stage sets for the gaudy tycoons of the Gilded Age. The first American architect to graduate from L'École des Beaux Arts and founder of the American Institute of Architects, Hunt had steeped himself in eclecticism. At Newport, Hunt built Belcourt for O. H. P. Belmont, Marble House for W. K. Vanderbilt and the Breakers for Cornelius Vanderbilt. The effect of Hunt's decoration of the 70-room Vanderbilt "cottage" with crystal chandeliers, marble fireplaces, gilt chairs and velvet curtains was, according to one visitor, "paralyzing."

America's academic architecture reached its zenith in 1893 at the World's Columbian Exposition in Chicago. This exposition reinforced the popularity of Revivalist architecture and, according to Louis Sullivan, "set American architecture back fifty years."

America Industrializes Architecture

Although building in the United States contributed modestly to conventional architecture in the last half of the 19th century, it added much to the technology of construction. Perhaps the most far-reaching contribution was the invention of the balloon-frame system of wood construction. Scholars still do not agree as to who was the inventor. Until recently most have attributed its invention to George Washington Snow, a surveyor and jack-of-all-trades. But some insist that the credit belongs to Augustine Taylor, a Hartford carpenter who became a builder in Chicago. Whoever the original inventor was, the new system revolutionized building, especially in the American West. Under the conventional system, carpenters had pegged posts to beams by means of hard-to-make mortise-and-tenon joints; the new system allowed them to nail boards to a frame, eliminating the need for artful joinery and substituting inexpensive machine-made metal nails for wooden pegs. Balloon framing thus converted building in wood from a complicated handcraft practiced by master carpenters to a prefabricated system assembled by unskilled laborers. The lightweight balloon frame (overleaf) cost 40 percent less than the conventional mortise-and-tenon frame and left the builder with capital to invest elsewhere.

McKim, Mead and White. Lowe House, Bristol, R.I. 1887

Conditions in Chicago of 1832 encouraged the birth of the balloon frame. With the end of the Black Hawk war in that year, Chicago mushroomed into a center for land speculation. Some property increased in value at the rate of 100 percent daily. As the population of the town shot from 200 in 1833 to 3,279 in 1835, the balloon frame presented itself as the solution to building needs. St. Mary's Church, the first balloon-frame structure on record, went up in 1833 at a cost of $900. By 1860, firms in Boston, Chicago and New York had begun to offer to ship prefabricated balloon-frame houses by rail to any point in the United States, thus marking the first step in the nation's prefabricated housing industry.

Richard Morris Hunt. The Breakers, Newport, R.I. 1895

Scarcely 15 years after the appearance of the wooden balloon frame, American designers began experimenting with cast-iron frames. As early as 1848, 15 years earlier than similar experiments in Europe, James Bogardus (1800–1874) designed a factory with a cast-iron skeleton. In this building, iron rather than masonry walls supported each floor. Using such prefabricated iron skeletons, Bogardus built warehouses, department stores and office buildings all over the United States between 1850 and 1880. His best-known building, an arch-fronted structure for the publishing house of Harper & Brothers, no longer stands, but similar buildings in New York, St. Louis and Chicago are still in use. A prolific inventor, Bogardus also patented an engraving machine that printed the first English postage stamps and a pencil whose lead was always sharp.

Richard Morris Hunt. Ochre Court, Newport, R.I. 1888–1889

With the cast-iron frame, another technological development appeared at mid-century to speed the advent of the skyscraper: the safety elevator. Mechanical hoisting platforms had been common, but they were not all that reliable. A safety device was invented by Elisha Graves Otis, who demonstrated it at the second Crystal Palace in New York in 1853. Four years after the demon-

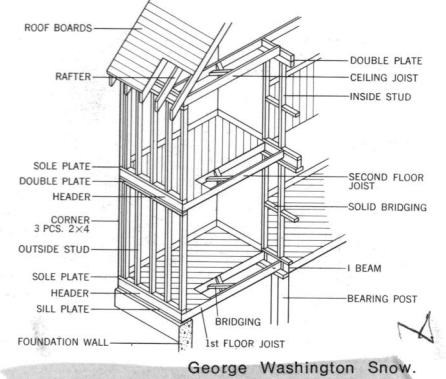

George Washington Snow.
Balloon frame construction, U.S.A. c. 1830

James Bogardus. Iron frame construction,
U.S.A. c. 1850

Elisha Otis. Safety elevator,
installed in Eiffel tower. 1887

stration, Otis installed an elevator in a department store on Broome Street in New York; in 1889 he installed an entire system of steam-driven elevators for the first time in a really tall structure—the Eiffel Tower. Four of them ran from the ground to the first platform, two more from the first to second platform, and two more to the top. Total ascent of 1,000 feet took seven minutes, and 2,350 passengers could be transported every hour. With the safety elevator and metal-frame construction available, architects would begin to build tall buildings which, together with the simple shingle homes of Richardson, exemplified the proto-Functionalist mode.

New York's Central Park (opposite) was important not because Frederick Law Olmsted (1822–1903) introduced a new style in landscape gardening, but because he was the first to conceive a park not as an aristocratic enclave but as a playground for the public and because of the excellence of the park's totally designed environment in which a planned visual experience awaited the visitor's every glance. His landscaping details themselves were in the Picturesque mode that had marked the English garden since Humphrey Repton laid out the grounds for Horace Walpole's Strawberry Hill in 1752.

Born in Hartford, the son of a merchant, Olmsted traveled extensively in America and Europe before settling down on a farm in South Side, Staten Island. In 1857 he became superintendent of Central Park, and the next year, working anonymously with a collaborator, he submitted the prize-winning plan for redesigning the park, which had existed for six years without any comprehensive plan.

In four years of construction and planting, Olmsted transformed 800 acres of barren pastureland, broken here and there by swamps and out-croppings of rock, into a place of beauty. The great park's programmed sequences of visual experience are flawed today in only one respect. Olmsted had bordered the park with rows of trees to shield the stroller from urban distractions. He could not foresee that giant buildings would one day tower behind the trees meant to protect his meticulously planned landscapes. An aerial photo of Central Park shows how industrial man has deified nature. Girdled by concrete and steel structures, the park has been enshrined in the center of the city like a medieval cathedral.

John A. Roebling (1806–1869), a German immigrant, combined Picturesque, neo-Gothic details with the most advanced engineering techniques of his time to build Brooklyn Bridge. To Roebling's fellow immigrants, the arches of the great bridge symbolized a continuity with past forms and with the Old World while its cables spoke of new forms and the New World. The poem "Brooklyn Bridge," which Hart Crane wrote a generation after John Roebling's death, is a testament to the abiding power of the great structure. "Thy cables breathe the North Atlantic still," Crane wrote.

Aerial view, Central Park

Raising the Obelisk, Central Park

Belvedere Castle, Central Park

Bethesda Fountain, Central Park

Ornamental fence, Central Park

Sculpted stairway, Central Park

Foot bridge, Central Park

Horse-drawn carriage on auto route, Central Park

Map showing depressed transverse auto routes, Central Park

John Roebling. Brooklyn Bridge,
New York. 1869–1883

Brooklyn Bridge. Weaving steel cable

Brooklyn Bridge. Wrapping the cable

The largest suspension bridge that had been built up to that time, it took a dozen years to complete and cost Roebling's life and the lives of twenty workmen. Injured in a ferry accident, Roebling died of lockjaw when construction of the bridge had barely begun. Washington Roebling, his son and ardent disciple, completed it.

The bridge could not have been built without the use of steel cables, which Roebling himself had invented in his early career as an engineer in Pennsylvania. Four huge cables, spun in mid-air from 5,000 strands of steel wire, safely carried the 3,500-foot roadbed of the bridge in the face of dire predictions from more cautious professionals. Curiously, these highly functional steel cables were suspended from 276-foot-high piers whose pointed arches were neo-Gothic.

The architectural critics of Roebling's own era damned the bridge's "barbaric" lack of ornament. Twentieth-century critics have deplored the revivalism of the neo-Gothic piers as an unfortunate lapse of taste on Roebling's part. In fact, the secret of the compelling interest of the structure is the dialectic between its Picturesque and proto-Functionalist elements. As no other monument, it embodies the tension between the two modes—the conflict between the practical and the ideal in the Victorian temperament. Its straight-lined, machine-spun cables speak, in the prose of engineering, for utility. Their harp-like beauty is the beauty of mathematical precision; their power is the power of mechanical invention. The hand-laid brick piers of the bridge speak, in the poetry of architecture, for art. Their lofty arches evoke Old World cathedrals; their spirituality is that of a time long gone. If style is a language and if the artifacts expressing themselves in that language are the metaphors of culture, then Brooklyn Bridge is the perfect metaphor for 19th-century America.

VICTORIAN FURNITURE AND INTERIOR DESIGN

In 1836 the French poet Alfred de Musset said, "We have left no imprint of our age either on our dwellings, on our gardens, or on anything else, we have culled something from every century but our own—we live off fragments." This was not completely true. Victorian furniture designers culled motifs from a succession of historic styles. But no matter what style, or combination of styles, the designer imitated, an unmistakably Victorian character emerged in the ultimate design. What was this character? It was superficial. In a literal sense, the Victorian furniture designer concentrated on the surface of a thing at the expense of structure. It was big: just as Victorian buildings grew in scale, so did chairs, beds and sideboards. It was ostentatious: in the England of Dickens, the America of Twain and the France of Balzac, new tycoons advertised their wealth with gaudy furnishings and homes.

In addition to the borrowing of motifs from Greek, Roman, Gothic and other historical styles, Victorian furniture exhibited other Picturesque elements. Most important was a peculiarly curved line. The Picturesque line links two concave curves together by means of a single convex one. This line silhouettes the sides of the chair designed by A. Jones for exhibit at the Crystal Palace. At its most luxurious, it imitates the outline of a violin or lyre. Lillian Russell, the actress, exemplified the line in her own silhouette. And every Victorian woman who could afford whalebone struggled to conform to it. The line rolls freely through the ascenders and descenders of Victorian type faces and bulges from the sides of the Coca-Cola bottle. With Art Nouveau, the two concave curves compress into a whiplash curve. That line snakes through the illustrations of Aubrey Beardsley and the typography of Otto Eckmann. By the 20th century a single concave curve, stretched into a parabola, replaced the Art-Nouveau whiplash. This curve outlines Maillart's Concrete Exposition Building (page 83) and forms Saarinen's Gateway Arch. Thus, each permutation of line reflected a permutation in style. From the Picturesque mode of Victorian design to the Curvilinear mode of Art Nouveau to the Expressionist mode of Modern design, each linear permutation evoked, successively, the fullness of the female body, the sinuosity of the reptile and the cold, celestial perfection of geometry. Polarized against these three curves was the straight line of proto-Functionalist Victorian, Rectilinear Art Nouveau and Functionalist Modern design. This line evoked the rationalism of the machine and, in its continuity through three stylistic stages, attested to the abiding attraction of the machine as a source for Modern forms.

The most curious aspect of Picturesque design is its penchant for narrative devices. Mottoes were cross-stitched into samplers, carved into chairs, engraved into silver-backed mirrors and embossed on china shaving mugs. Dog-

A. Jones. Chair. This and all furniture, pages 25–27, from Crystal Palace exhibits, London. 1851

H. Fitz Cook, *Daydreamer* chair, London. 1851

R. W. Wingfield. Or-Molu cot, London. 1851

Craydon. Crusader chess table, London. 1851

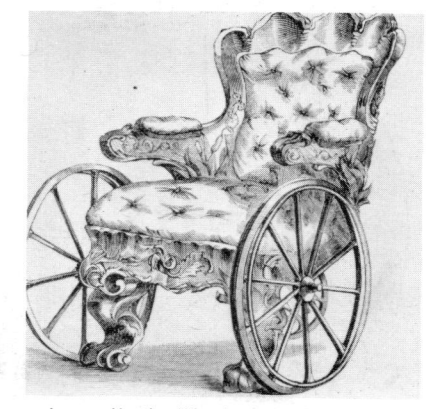

James Heath. Wheel chair, London. 1851

like arms inspired Jones of Dublin to carve on the back of his chair the motto: "Gentle when stroked, angry when provoked." Whatever the explanation for the story-telling penchant, it is congruent with the novel (a long story) and the opera (a story set to music).

The Daydreamer (page 25), a favorite chair exhibited at the Crystal Palace, incorporated all the elements that characterize the Picturesque mode in furniture. Its lines were curved rather than straight, its legs terminating in a rococo curve rather than being conventionally at right angles with the seat. Its entire surface was ornamented with angels, snowdrops and poppies. Its texture was concealed beneath incised lines. To explain the allegory they presented, manufacturers of the Daydreamer accompanied it with a long explanation: "The chair is decorated at the top with two winged thoughts—the one with bird-like pinions, and crowned with roses, representing joyous dreams, the other with leather bat-like wings—unpleasant and troubled ones. Behind is displayed Hope, under the figure of the rising sun . . . The style is Italian." The designer executed this elaborate allegory with utter literalness. The penchant for literally portraying non-real allegories and fantasies also characterizes the paintings of Millais, Burne-Jones, W. H. Hunt and other pre-Raphaelites. This suggests that designers and painters worked under a mutual influence. Photography, with its unmatchable verisimilitude, offered a quality which the painters and designers tried to rival.

The Daydreamer, like the Houses of Parliament, was costumed in historic garb. Yet, when its manufacturer said, "The style is Italian," he did not designate a specific period nor had he incorporated details that were any more Italian than French. But reviving historic motifs while disregarding historical accuracy was an overriding characteristic of the Picturesque mode. Even when Pugin, Jones and other Victorian designers educated themselves in the characteristics of a historic style, the harp-like curve, the broken outline, the busy surface and the literalness of the Picturesque mode overpowered the copied one.

Not creative bankruptcy but a yearning to express himself compelled the Daydreamer's designer to carve his fantasies into his furniture. As for the purchaser, having bought the chair he could turn back the pointed hands of his neo-Gothic clock to a time when men were knights, not office clerks, and hope that his child, slumbering in his scalloped pseudo-Italian crib, need never engage in the harsh business of business.

The Crystal Palace provided an extraordinary showcase for Victorian furniture, and the items on pages 25 to 27 all appeared on display there. M. Roule's bedstead, "a free and fanciful work in the Italian style," according to the exhibition catalog, was but one of many dizzy experiments in form. Other display pieces confirm the Victorian designer's passion for experimentation—however misguided—with new materials. H. Fitz Cook, for example, fashioned the Day-dreamer in papier-mâché rather than wood. A designer named Clay entered in the exhibit a dressing table and chair also made of papier-mâché. Wicker furniture, such as the chair designed by John Tuph of New York, was another novelty. Michael Thonet, in a few years to become world famous for mass-produced bentwood side chairs and rockers (page 68), had already begun to experiment with bentwood in 1851 and entered a table produced by that process. Other furniture makers exhibited furniture made of iron, zinc and even rubber, all either new materials or, in the case of iron, more readily available than ever before.

M. Roule. Bedstead in Italian style, London. 1851

H. Clay. Dressing table and chair, papier-mâché, England. 1851

John Tuph. Wicker chair, New York. 1851

Collard & Collard. Upright piano. England. 1851

A. W. N. Pugin. Bookcase in Gothic style. England. 1851

Michael Thonet. Table with bentwood legs. 1851

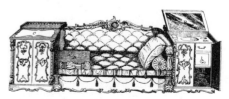

Taylor & Sons. Steamship furniture convertible into life raft. England. 1851

Philip Webb. Red House, England. 1859

Philip Webb and William Morris.
Red House interior, England. 1860

Warrington Taylor after Ephraim Coleman.
"Morris" chair, England. c. 1862

Victorian designers were also intrigued by the possibilities of simulating one material with another. They painted slabs of glass to resemble marble, pine to resemble oak and electro-plated zinc to resemble sterling silver. This practice illustrates an important difference between Victorian and Modern values. While contemporary critics have praised Eero Saarinen's "honesty" in leaving the concrete surfaces of New York's TWA Terminal unfinished to reveal its nature and the nature of the forming process, Victorians admired the skill with which A. J. Davis painted the canvas-walled interiors of Lyndhurst to resemble ashlar stonework.

Multi-purpose furniture was another interest of the Victorian designers. Hence, the British firm Taylor and Sons introduced at the Crystal Palace a steamship sofa that converted into a life-raft. Working along similar lines, R. W. Laurie showed a portmanteau (page 35) that converted into a life-raft.

Pugin, of course, saw the Crystal Palace as a splendid opportunity to promote the Gothic Revival and designed a Medieval Court to display religious and secular furnishings, among them a bookcase, in the neo-Gothic manner. Such furniture directly influenced the American architect A. J. Davis, who followed Pugin's sketches in the design of neo-Gothic chairs (page 30) and tables to complement the neo-Gothic exterior of Lyndhurst. Richard Morris Hunt selected similar pieces to furnish a Gothic Room for Marble House (page 30) in Newport.

Henry Cole, the Reformer

Innocuously quaint as the furniture at the Crystal Palace appears today, in 1851 it was the subject of serious concern. Soon after the Great Exhibition opened, *The Times* of London commented: "The absence of any fixed principles in ornamental design is apparent in the Exhibition—it seems to us that the art manufacturers of the whole of Europe are thoroughly demoralized." Even before the Exhibition opened, the collapse of British design standards had concerned Henry Cole (1802–1882). Neither a manufacturer nor a designer, Cole was a civil servant who spotlighted the importance of design through annual exhibitions at London's Society of Arts.

In 1849 he founded the *Journal of Design* to promote the idea that good design is good business. In the *Journal* Cole reported on all kinds of products. Lacking the term "industrial design" he coined the term "art manufacture." By this Cole meant "fine art or beauty applied to mechanical production." Most important, Cole launched the Great Exhibition by persuading Prince Albert, then president of the Society of Arts, to back it. Already concerned about the absence of design and production standards in machine-based British industry, Cole wanted to dramatize this failure. The Exhibition proved that the new machine-made goods were inferior to handcrafted ones, but, unfortunately, created the impression that this was inherent in the machine-production process rather than in how the process was used.

Quest for an Earthly Paradise

William Morris (1834–1896) was among those left with a negative impression of machine-made goods. Like Cole, Morris recognized the failure of the new mechanized industrial system to produce well-designed furniture. But, unlike Cole, Morris urged the revival of handcraft production and a return to Gothic style. This alternative was not only regressive but impractical.

H. Brinton. Carpet, England. 1851

In 1859 Morris married the beautiful Jane Burden and in the following year built Red House. Though neo-Gothic in pointed windows and peaked roofs, Red House was proto-Functionalist in floor plan—the kitchen was placed on the ground floor rather than in the basement—and in reliance on texture rather than ornament for visual interest. Philip Webb, who designed Red House, attempted to apply the same high standard to its furnishings as to its architecture.

Distressed by the difficulty of finding appropriate furnishings, Morris, in 1861, decided to form his own design and manufacturing firm. It produced wallpaper, glassware, wall hangings, jewelry, fabrics and furniture, and included the pre-Raphaelites Burne-Jones, Rossetti and Ford Madox Brown among its partners. By surrounding himself and others with the firm's work, Morris sought, as the name of one of his poems suggests, to make the world an "earthly paradise." His mistake was in believing it could be done by reviving the Gothic style.

William Morris. Lily carpet, England. 1877

Morris's most successful designs were flat, well-organized patterns for fabrics, carpets and wallpapers—all more sophisticated than the fabrics at the Crystal Palace. The popular Morris chair was not designed by Morris but by Warington Taylor, the young manager of his firm. Taylor apparently copied both the adjustable back and the overall form from Ephraim Coleman, an English furniture maker.

Interestingly, Morris's work failed to conform to many of his doctrines, for which he is also famous. He preached socialism, yet his designs were for the houses of rich men. He revived the decorative arts, yet refused to utilize mechanized means of producing them. Ironically, the reform in taste that he sought was advanced by manufacturers who plagiarized his designs and distributed them to people of all classes by means of the mass-production system he despised. Yet it was the success of his firm—Morris, Marshall, Faulkner and

William Morris. Carpet, England. c. 1870

29

Anonymous. Milligan house, interior, Saratoga, N.Y. 1850–1856

R. M. Hunt. Gothic room, Marble house, Newport, R.I. 1888–1890

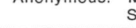

A. J. Davis. Neo-Gothic chair, New York. 1840–1847

Company—that taught other manufacturers that money could be made from good design. Though it was not his intention, Morris created the demand in industry for a new kind of professional—the industrial designer.

America's Brown Decades

During most of the 19th century, American furniture followed English fashion slavishly. The British tastemaker John Lock Eastlake (1820–1890) influenced American chair design with his straight-sided neo-Gothic chairs and with *Hints on Household Taste,* in which he emphasized function as well as neo-Gothic forms. What had seemed amusing naiveté in British revivalist furniture became plodding vulgarity in many American imitations. One reason was public ignorance. Important books were ignored—*Moby Dick, The Scarlet Letter* and *Walden,* all published about when the Crystal Palace opened, went unnoticed. Serious designers could just as well not have existed. A Roebling, a Richardson, a Sullivan, a LaFarge "were men that any age might proudly exhibit," said Lewis Mumford in *The Brown Decades,* "but the procession of American civilization divided and walked around these men."

Ostentation rather than function governed American interim design between mid-century and the Civil War. The gaudy red-and-gold color scheme of the Milligan House drawing-room spelled dollars, not delight, conspicuous consumption, not comfort. But by 1865 the long shadow of the Civil War fell over the American home. Gold and red faded into brown, russet and forest green. The death of Abraham Lincoln in 1865 signaled a period of mourning for the 617,528 dead, and portraits of dead husbands, dead fathers, dead brothers, dead lovers haunted the parlor of the American home. White woodwork was stained brown. Walnut furniture replaced rosewood and mahogany. Richardson's brown shingle houses darkened the countryside and brownstone covered the red-brick façades of city homes. The brown decades had arrived.

Although most American chairs were an insensitive copy of some historic style, those coming from the inventor rather than the furniture-maker were full of utilitarian novelty. From 1850 to 1900 hundreds of ideas for swivel chairs, collapsible chairs, folding beds and convertible tables were registered at the U. S. Patent Office. Among the striking proto-Functionalist examples were a reclining railroad seat, prototype of today's airplane seat, and an adjustable barber's chair, prototype for today's dentist chair.

Designer John Henry Belter, a German immigrant who popularized rosewood in New York, took out a secret patent process in 1856 to make what seemed to be conventional hand-carved chairs. Although the Egyptians had invented wood lamination, Belter, along with the German furniture maker Michael

Thonet, pioneered 19th-century experiments with the process. Belter planed down layers of rosewood to 1/16 of an inch and then sandpapered them to a satin finish. He glued together as many as 16 layers at right angles to one another for a total thickness of no more than an inch. By steaming this plywood sandwich in a mold, Belter made concave chair-backs out of a single sandwich. Only laminated wood possessed sufficient strength for the flower and foliage openwork Belter carved into his chairs. Ironically, Belter turned his highly original technology to the production of stylistically conservative chairs. Legend says that he dramatized to customers the strength of his imitation Louis XV chairs by throwing them from the top floor window of his Third Avenue workshop. Shortly before his death, Belter destroyed his patterns and molds, and his expensive but popular furniture disappeared from New York drawing rooms. It was not until two generations later, with the plywood chairs of Alvar Aalto, that laminated wooden chairs reappeared.

Like the Belter chair, the Wooton desk combined technological innovation with neo-Gothic styling of marked conservatism. Before William S. Wooton patented his design in 1874, the typical secretary desk had a lower section with drawers, a drop-front that served as writing surface, a top section consisting of pigeonholes and a bookcase, enclosed by glass doors. Wooton's desk combined these elements in a single center section, which, in addition, had seven secret compartments. At a time when public banks were both rare and unreliable, these secret compartments provided owners with a private bank. Wooton installed in each of two deep doors more than two dozen convenient pigeonholes. As the nation converted from agriculture to commerce, the Wooton desk became a symbol of status. Jay Gould, Joseph Pulitzer and John D. Rockefeller bought Wooton desks. They looked solid and expensive, and at $255 each, they were.

American Chair Company. Swivel chair, New York. 1851

John Belter. Louis XV plywood chair, New York. c. 1860

William S. Wooton. Neo-gothic patented desk, New York. 1874

Joseph Bramah. Water closet. England. 1877

Anonymous. Dolphin water closet, U.S.A. c. 1890

Eugene Viollet-le-Duc. Neo-gothic sink,
France. c. 1851

Furniture for the Bath

In the years after 1880 manufacturers applied mass-production techniques to the making of bathroom fixtures as well as furniture. However, the addition of a bathroom to the Victorian home involved a long battle. President Millard Fillmore's installation of a bathtub in the White House in 1851 met with outraged criticism, and it was not until 1877, during the residency of Rutherford B. Hayes, that tubs with running water were installed. Between 1854 and 1862 it was unlawful in Boston to bathe except on a doctor's advice. In the 1880's only one American home in six had a bathtub.

Early furniture for the bath was engineered rather than styled. The first valve-operated water closet, patented by the Englishman Joseph Bramah in 1777, was as functional and undecorated as would be the McCormick reaper (page 33). Only with the mass marketing of toilets and tubs a century later did public taste influence design. Thus, the Dolphin water closet, though engineered like the Bramah closet, was styled in the Picturesque manner. Neo-Gothic open-work pull-chair and neo-Renaissance base infused this humble artifact with elegance. Viollet-le-Duc, who was to become the architectural restorer of Notre Dame Cathedral, designed the Fontaine Lavabo in the neo-Gothic manner. Water could not at that time be pumped in, so it was retained in a castle-faced reservoir and released into what appeared to be a baptismal font.

VICTORIAN INDUSTRIAL DESIGN

Until the 19th century, man had surrounded himself with relatively few things—chairs, tables, chests, cooking utensils, the tools of the trades, the tools of war, a few scientific instruments and some toys. But between 1790 and 1900, 600,000 patents for new devices were granted in the United States alone. Many of them covered machines that would transform the farm, the office and the home. Locomotives, steamships and bicycles led to mechanized transportation. The typewriter, the adding machine, the cash register, the dictaphone and the telephone—each introduced between 1875 and 1900—mechanized office work. Factory canning, factory baking, the washing machine and the sewing machine simplified, if they did not mechanize, housework. "Things," as Ralph Waldo Emerson had it, "are in the saddle, and ride mankind." The question was: what should each thing look like?

George Angell. Silver flagons. This and all products, pages 33–35, Crystal Palace exhibits, London. 1851

The variety of design solutions arrived at for the staggering array of objects, such as all those shown on pages 33 to 35, exhibited at the Crystal Palace attested to the lack of consensus on the answer to this question. It was clear that the industrial designer faced the same question as the architect. Should he clothe his new product in an historic costume, or should he forge a new style for machine-made products? Most elected the former. Following the esthetic of the Picturesque, product designers turned to past styles or to nature as a source for forms.

Thus George Angell sought to evoke the spirituality of the 14th century by designing a flagon after Gothic models. That the tortured curve in the handle makes it awkward to hold and that the encrusted surface makes it difficult to clean were secondary to Angell. The Picturesque mode even penetrated the Hall of Machines, where one hydraulic press was executed in sober neo-Egyptian, deemed appropriate to the serious business of manufacture. The use of historical styles was not the only Picturesque note at the Crystal Palace. Other Picturesque elements cropped up in the products on display: stories were incorporated into designs and executed with excruciating literalness, surfaces were ornamented and the ubiquitous Picturesque curve was greatly favored.

B. Hick and Son. Engine in "the Egyptian taste," London. 1851

Debut of the Machine Style

Despite the regressive historicism of the majority of designers, a few responded to the conversion from hand- to machine-production by adapting to the new technology and by evolving an appropriate style for it; inventors, in their apparently styleless patent models, introduced the Modern look before

Cyrus McCormick, Mechanical reaping machine, U.S.A. Patent, 1835

Henry Cole. Teaset for Minton's, England. 1851

Garrard's. Emperor of Russia's ewer, London. 1851

Charles Avisseau. Fruit dish, England. 1851

practicing product designers did.

Among the American entries at the Crystal Palace, Cyrus McCormick's Patent Virginia Reaper and Samuel Colt's revolver carried off prizes for performance. But simplicity of appearance made the reaper a public joke. So stark and apparently non-styled was the reaper, compared to other farm equipment on display, that *The Times* of London dubbed it "a cross between an Astley chariot, a wheel barrow, and a flying machine." When in a contest against other mechanical reapers, McCormick's cut at a speed of 20 acres a day, *The Times* contritely reported that "the reaping machine from the United States is the most valuable contribution from abroad to the stock of our previous knowledge we have yet discovered."

The simplicity of the Colt revolver (page 36) contrasted dramatically with floridly engraved, handcrafted weapons from France and England and Tiffany in the United States. The British were impressed by the performance of this weapon. Patented in 1832, it was the first commercially successful automatic pistol, firing at first five, and later six shots in succession without reloading. They were amazed by Colt's method of mass-production manufacture in which die-cutting machines duplicated each part. At the invitation of the British Institute of Civil Engineers, Colt set up in England a factory similar to his American factory.

Not only could Colt's machines stamp out a part many times faster than the human hand could fashion it, but each part was reproduced with sufficient precision to make it interchangeable with the same part from another unit. This system, developed by Eli Whitney and other inventors, is one of two key elements in the mass-production process.

The second element is the assembly of interchangeable parts into completed units on a continuously moving automatic assembly line. Oliver Evans, a Philadelphia inventor, introduced the first automatic assembly line into his flour mill in 1785. Combining an Archimedes' screw and a chain of buckets with an endless belt, Evans processed three bushels of grain an hour. The mill required no human labor from the time grain was unloaded until it was ground into flour. Meat processors, such as the hog butchers of Cincinnati, also introduced assembly-line techniques in the dressing of meat.

Simplifying the shape of a product in order to simplify the means of its manufacture grew directly from the new mass-production system. This system was soon adopted by manufacturers of sewing machines, watches, locomotives and bicycles. That simplification of form became a question of style as well as a question of production technique is indicated by the fact that the same machines could and did turn out products in the complexly curved Picturesque mode as well as in the proto-Functionalist mode. Styling was dictated not only by considerations of production efficiency but also by esthetic

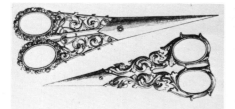

W. Thornhill. Scissors, London. 1851

Anonymous. Fork and spoon, London. 1851

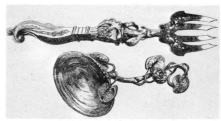

F. Higgins. Fish fork and cream ladle, London. 1851

Hiram Powers. *Greek Slave*, London. 1851

John Bell. *Andromeda*, London. 1851

John Bell. *Dorothea*, London. 1851

Raffaele Monti. *Circassian Slave*, London. 1851

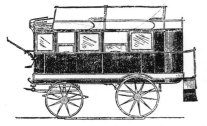

J. A. Franklinski. Omnibus, London. 1851

R. W. Laurie. Portmanteau convertible to life preserver, London. 1851

Hallmarke & Aldebert. Underspring step-piece barouche, London. 1851

considerations—the esthetic acceptability of a product to the buyers and to the factory owners themselves. It was less machine production than divergent taste that accounted for both the Gothic-arched cab windows of the Auburn locomotive and the straight-lined frame of the Columbia bicycle. While the mass production system provided the basis for a new machine esthetic, which was ultimately to replace the bankrupt esthetic of the Picturesque, the new esthetic would not even be recognized by design historians until after World War I.

Samuel Colt. Single-action .44 revolver, U.S.A. 1875; original patent, 1835

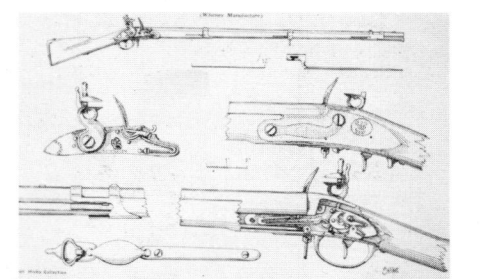

Eli Whitney. Rifle parts produced by interchangeable parts manufacturing system, U.S.A. 1879

Cincinnati slaughterhouse production line, U.S.A. c. 1860

Unanswered Questions

It is a measure of industry's lack of concern for good design that most manufacturers failed to record the names of the designers of their products during the Victorian period. Who were George Angell and the other designers whose names appear in the catalog for the Great Exhibition? The names of Edison, Bell and others who patented new products are recorded, but names of the designers who styled the phonograph, the telephone and the typewriter are not. Neither the Bell Company nor Western Electric has a record of a designer between 1877, when Bell introduced the first commercial model, and 1936, when Western Electric, the actual manufacturer of later models, retained Henry Dreyfuss as consultant designer. The Edison National Historic Site records Edison's patent model phonograph, his sketches, even his conversations. It does not name the designers who changed housing, horn shape, materials and graphics in the dozens of phonographs following the patent model of 1877.

As serious as the lack of information about Victorian designers is the absence of a museum collection of Victorian design. The Smithsonian Institution exhibits Victorian inventions, but it collects on the basis of technological rather than stylistic significance. The Museum of Modern Art exhibits Art Nouveau design but considers Victorian artifacts out-of-bounds. The Victoria and Albert Museum exhibits Victorian furniture but few Victorian products.

While the history of Victorian architecture and photography has been documented by professional historians, the history of Victorian furniture and graphic design has scarcely been recorded. The British critic John Gloag relates Victorian furniture to British social history. He does not place it in the context of an emerging Modern style. Most histories of typography, such as A. F. Johnson's *Type Design,* terminate around 1820, just before the first examples of Modern typography appear.

Many questions must be answered by future Victorian-design scholars. How significantly did machine production modify product design in the Victorian period? Machine-stamping and die-casting of parts are said to have encouraged simpler forms and smoother surfaces. But were such processes the most influential factor in modifying form? Or was the machine—as a stylistic source for forms—more influential? In short, what was the relationship between the designer's drive to express form and the enhancement or limitation of that drive by machine production?

How did merchandising influence Victorian product design? Was it, as seems likely, a more potent factor in the looks of the cash register, the sewing machine and other consumer products than was mass production? Since the 1940's, styling has played a more important role in autos, toasters and TV sets than in electronic equipment or medical instruments. For the same reasons, did styling play a more important role in Victorian housewares and furniture than in farm implements?

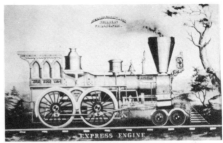
Richard Morris and Son. Auburn locomotive, Philadelphia. 1854

The Evolving Telephone

Although the esthetic that governs the architect also governs the product designer, the problems of the two are different. The architect creates a building where none existed. The product designer seeks an appropriate form for someone else's invention. The architect designs a building out of parts—whether wood, brick or iron—whose form and behavior he knows in advance. The product designer bends the form of his product to suit the means of production—whether molding, stamping, extruding, spinning or die-casting. The architect, at least in the 19th century, built for permanence. A product designer typically creates for the moment. A second designer may later modify the original product with better engineering, new materials or a change in styling. Thus the design of a product evolves. That of a building does not.

The Columbia Racing Safety.
Weight, 23 lbs.
Anonymous. Columbia bicycle, U.S.A. c. 1888–1890

Evolution in a product, as the development of the telephone (page 38) indicates, more often means improved engineering than improved form. Each of the 28 models introduced by the Bell Telephone Company between 1877 (when its first commercial telephone appeared) and 1965 incorporated significant engineering improvements. The wall set of 1882 provided a transmitter that was separated from the receiver. The 1897 set was far smaller and lighter than the big set of 1882 and could be placed on a desk for convenience. The 1937 desk set substituted plastic for metal. The 1965 trimline model combined receiver, transmitter and dial in a single element. That these models have been styled, as well as engineered, is obvious. A designer has arbitrarily straightened the Lillian-Russell curves of the 1897 model in the model of 1900. Yet, with the exception of the 1882 set and of the trimline, not one of these models stands out in terms of form. The form of the 1877 set tells nothing of its function. The straight-lined receiver of the 1897 set is incompatible with the curves of

Anonymous. Edison phonographs, U.S.A. 1890–1910

Alexander Graham Bell. First commercial model phone, U.S.A. 1877

Alexander Graham Bell. Butterstamp model, U.S.A. 1878

Alexander Graham Bell. Wall model, U.S.A. 1878

Francis Blake, Jr. Improved transmitter combined with Bell's receiver, U.S.A. 1882

Staff design. Desk model, U.S.A. 1897

Staff design. Desk model, U.S.A. c. 1916

Henry Dreyfuss. ''300'' desk model, U.S.A. 1937

Henry Dreyfuss and Western Electric staff. Desk model, U.S.A. 1949

Western Electric staff. Trimline model, U.S.A. 1965

the base. The 1937 set vacillates between articulating its function and concealing it in an envelope. Factory production fragmented the fabrication process, and design (meaning style) and design (meaning engineering) separated into two different activities. This separation helps explain why successive models of the telephone have failed in terms of form.

The cash register had a somewhat more successful design history than the telephone. From the time James Ritty patented the first model in 1878, until 1881 when he finished the fourth model, the Dayton café owner made successive improvements in mechanical operation. But he made no attempt at styling. Then in 1881 Ritty sold the cash register to what was to become the National Cash Register Company. In 1883, when NCR sold the first cash register to the public, it also retained its first stylist, an unknown German cabinet-maker who carved flowers and the firm's initials into the machine's wooden front. The model of 1890, the first able to provide a cumulative total of individual transactions, kept the shape of the prior model, but surface decoration spread from a panel above the keys to the side and back surfaces. Since this model brought increased sales, NCR switched from a hand-made wooden cabinet to a machine-produced metal cabinet whose color, appropriately, was gold. By 1900 the cash register had evolved into a unified and consistent example of Picturesque design, while the telephone's awkwardly unrelated forms were still being made in contrasting wood and metal parts.

James Ritty. Cash register, U.S.A. 1881

Anonymous. National Cash Register, first commercial model, U.S.A. 1883

Anonymous. National Cash Register metal model, U.S.A. 1890

P. T. Barnum. Poster, U.S.A. c. 1860
Anonymous. Advertisements, U.S.A. c. 1890

How far, O Catiline, wilt tho
How long shall thy frantic ra
Justice? To what height mea
daring insolence? Art thou n
nocturnal host to secure the 1
the City Guards? ABCDEFGHI
ABCDEFGHIJKLMNOPQ

How far, O Catiline, wilt tho
How long shall thy frantic ra
Justice? To what height mea
daring insolence? Art thou n
ABCDEFGHIJKLMNOPQRSTU
ABCDEFGHIJKLMNOP

Robert Thorne. Fat face, London. 1804

VICTORIAN GRAPHIC DESIGN

Victorian graphics paralleled Victorian furniture and products in style. As drawing rooms had grown stuffy with furniture, so layouts became crowded. Teaspoons sprouted cabbage roses and so did type faces. Buildings and type sizes grew larger. Chair legs began to bulge, and type faces followed suit. Formerly straight-sided letters grew fat and were called, aptly, fat faces. Robert Thorne designed the first fat-faced letter, large and rounded like the bustles of the 1860's, in 1803 for the Fann Street Foundry in London. For most Victorian typographers, legibility counted far less than show. With this face the Picturesque mode in typography begins.

Literalness had been an important element in the Picturesque chair, and it became important in typography. Three-dimensional shadow letters with entire scenes cut into them grew naturally from Thorne's fat faces. Appalled by these travesties on the medieval monk's illuminated initial letter, one conservative old printer exclaimed: "The chaste and dignified black letter and Old Face sprouted horns and were dishonored. They bellied out to obesity, they were eviscerated and herring-gutted; they thickened to Dorics, shrieked to hysterics, shrank to hairlines. The world of Caslon and Baskerville, Janson and Bodoni and Aldus became the world of Caliban."

Although printers first used the fat faces and shadow letters for lottery tickets and theatrical posters, Phineas Taylor Barnum, famed and fabled founder of the Barnum and Bailey circus, pressed them to more strident extremes. He designed no faces but exploited fat faces so successfully in posters advertising his shows that printers and typographers still associate these faces with his name.

The Gothic Revival permeated Picturesque typography as it had Picturesque architecture. Having fallen into disuse, Gothic type faces were revived by the 1850's for handbills, posters and shipping schedules. William Morris, the furniture designer, helped popularize Gothic faces. To protest against the excesses in typography, Morris founded the Kelmscott Press in 1890. Hoping to design books that would be beautiful as well as easy to read, he succeeded only in the former. The Kelmscott *Chaucer,* luxuriantly decorated and illustrated, was called "the most beautiful book in the world," but, printed in Morris's Golden type, it was as difficult to read as his other books. His three new faces—Golden, Troy and Chaucer—were more like Gothic hand lettering than anything designed for a modern press. When the press closed after his death in 1896, 53 books had been designed and published. Beautiful in a precious way, they had as little to do with the impending 20th century as did Morris's essentially regressive philosophy of handcraftsmanship.

With the influence of historicism, Egyptian type also flourished. Robert

Thorne designed the first version in 1815 to meet the demand for bold advertising faces. Rival typographers Vincent Figgins and Edmund Fry showed a specimen version in 1820. In selecting the fashionable word "Egyptian" for a type face, Thorne reflected the Victorian interest in things Egyptian that had been stimulated by Napoleon's 1801 campaign in Egypt. Napoleon's architects, Percier and Fontaine, had used sphinxes and hieroglyphics to evoke Egypt in their furniture. With similar intention, Thorne devised a heavily monumental slab serif to call up Karnak and Abu Simbel. Egyptian type face met the new demand for bold letters and echoed the new scale and vigorous exaggeration of architecture. Several variations were designed in the 1830's and 1840's, and by 1860 Egyptian faces had become popular for theatrical posters. They were also used, in bold face, for dictionary heads. Contemporary variations, such as Memphis Girder, have been used for typewriter faces.

Proto-Functionalist Typography

Sans serif (page 42), the first proto-Functionalist type face, contrasted dramatically with the flood of new faces in the Picturesque mode. Although associated with the streamlined 1920's, sans serif was actually designed in 1816 by English typographer William Caslon IV and marks the first intrusion of the spirit of modern technology upon typography. Like Paxton's design for the Crystal Palace, sans serif helped create a taste for the proto-Functional. Caslon cut his original sans serif design in a single small size, and not until Vincent Figgins came out with a cruder but much larger version in 1832 did it become popular as a display type. By the 1850's the English printing trade had decided that sans serif was of greater merit for aggressive advertising than the popular fat faces. But not until 1916, when Edward Johnston, a British letterer and calligrapher, designed a version of sans serif for the British Underground Railway, was its proto-Functionalist flavor appreciated. With sans serif, typographers and designers made the mistake of confusing the proto-Functionalist look with function as a criterion of excellence. Insisting that sans serif made for a functional—that is, legible—face, they ignored laboratory reading tests proving the superior legibility of serifed type.

The Steam-Powered Press

Steam power, the driving force of the factory system, also revolutionized printing methods. Koenig's flatbed, steam-driven press ran for the first time on November 29, 1814, when *The Times* of London proudly announced that the

William Morris. Kelmscott Chaucer, England. 1890–1896

This is the Golden type.
This is the Troy type.
This is the Chaucer type.

William Morris. Golden, Troy and Chaucer type faces, England. 1890–1896

Quosque tandem abutere Catilina patientia FURNITURE 1820

Quosque tandem abutere Catilina patientia nostra? quamdiu nos W. THOROWGOOD.

Robert Thorne. Egyptian type face, England. 1815

Vincent Figgins. Sans serif type face, London. 1832

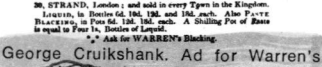

George Cruikshank. Ad for Warren's shoeblacking, England. c. 1820

Anonymous. Philadelphia *Chronicle*, U.S.A. 1831

issue in the reader's hand was the "result of the greatest improvement connected with printing since the discovery of the art itself." Fifty-five years later, *The Times* announced a second advance in its printing methods—this time the Walter Press. Prototype of the modern newspaper press, it printed a continuous roll of paper from curved stereotypes or cast plates. In the following decade Richard Hoe of New York developed the first web press. It delivered the paper folded, and turned out up to 18,000 impressions an hour—15,000 an hour more than the flatbed press. Ottmar Mergenthaler's invention of Linotype in 1884 and Tolbert Lanston's invention of monotype in 1885 also improved printing technology. Frederick Ives of Philadelphia completed the revolution in printing when he patented the crossline screen, or halftone, that made possible the printing of photographs.

New Design Media

As a growing system of mass production poured new products onto the market, manufacturers sold them increasingly through newspaper advertising. Still, newspaper publishers remained wedded to the most conservative design. They gave advertisements the same stingy look at mid-century as they had given them 50 years before and even forbade headlines larger than 8-point. Only rarely did they specify display type or white space to set off text. They discouraged any deviation from their standard format in the curious belief that allowing an ad to call attention to itself through unique design would be unfair to other advertisers. Besides, publishers thought there was more prestige in running several small ads than in running a single large one. To make their point, they charged advertisers extra for large type or broken column rules.

As for illustrations, only the Philadelphia *Chronicle* among American newspapers published more than occasional poorly printed thumbnail cuts. The 75-line, single-column advertisement for Warren's Shoe Blacking, illustrated by the caricaturist Cruikshank, began appearing in British literary weeklies around 1820. Because it was among the first ads to include an illustration, it made Warren's Shoe Blacking famous throughout the British Isles and marked the first time a professional artist had lent his talents to advertising.

From the beginning of the 19th century, graphic design played a more important role in magazines than in newspapers. *Godey's Lady's Book* did new fashions with colored steel engravings; *Harper's* converted Mathew Brady's war photographs into engravings and published Winslow Homer's sketches of the Civil War. *Leslie's Weekly* published Thomas Nast's cartoons on the same subject. After the war Nast's cartoons helped smash the Tweed Ring, and his tiger, donkey and elephant became permanent political symbols.

The Warner Corset Company, which began advertising soon after 1872, was one of the first manufacturers to use illustrations prominently in magazine advertising. The corset shaped the Victorian woman into the same Picturesque contours designers had imposed on type faces and teaspoons. Advertisements for Dr. Warner's corset sometimes showed entire drawing rooms in which the hour-glass figures of all the ladies were obviously due to the garment's forming effect.

Posters remained the most colorful advertising and design medium, untrammeled by the conservatism that afflicted the newspapers. Although posters had been published as early as 1845, they became important only after the 1870's, when French artists made them into a new art form.

Anonymous. Engraving showing poster display in train terminal, London. 1870's

Folk Art from the Merchant

The package provided the most colorful and—embellished as it was with family portraits, exposition medals and heraldic devices—the most memorable example of Victorian graphics. The familiar American packages shown here raise the question of the identity of the Victorian package designer. One assumes he was often the manufacturer or the printer's shop assistant, but the names of most of the Victorian package designers are lost to history.

Age lends nostalgic warmth to the Ballantine Beer and Bull Durham labels. Some manufacturers—for example, Anheuser-Busch and Lea and Perrins—find this quality so valuable that they guard against any package change. On the other hand, the Quaker Oats man, through repeated redesign, has become a bland shadow of his stern former self. Ivory's man in the moon has vanished. Coca-Cola, Campbell's Soup and Smith Brothers have simplified the original design of their packages while retaining their essential personality. The Coca-Cola bottle now comes in several sizes and its signature has been painted white, but it retains its Picturesque curve. The basically unchanged Campbell's Soup can, memorialized in Andy Warhol's Pop paintings of the 1960's, reverses the usual pattern in which painting influences packaging and suggests that package design influences painting.

Nostalgia alone does not account for the attraction of Victorian packages. Individuality, flamboyance and lack of self-consciousness add to their appeal. Contemporary package designers forfeit precisely these qualities when market researchers dictate to them that one menthol-cigarette package should imitate the green of a competing firm and that one cake-mix manufacturer should take a slice from a rival's cake package.

Individuality is the greatest strength of Victorian graphic design. While the trademarks of the 1960's are either difficult-to-remember abstract symbols or

Anonymous. Poster for Clipper ship, U.S.A. c. 1850

Anonymous. Ad for Warner Brothers, U.S.A. c. 1890

Anonymous. Quaker Oats, U.S.A. 1877
Jim Nash. Quaker Oats, U.S.A. 1945

difficult-to-read letter forms, the Victorian mark portrays the manufacturer's face, his wife's face or his factory. Not beautiful, perhaps, but unforgettable.

Whereas the designer of the Campbell's Soup can influenced paintings of the 1960's, the designers of the 1960's were influenced by the Abstract Expressionist painters of the 1950's. Abstraction made for a powerful school of painting but for uninteresting trademark design.

How much richer were the Victorian trademarks and packages. They have filled the mind with a pantheon of memorable personalities—the Smith Brothers, Baker's La Belle Chocolataire, Lydia E. Pinkham, King C. Gillette. In an age that worships fact, they are figures for a new industrial mythology.

Anonymous. Campbell's Soup can, U.S.A. 1894
Anonymous. Campbell's Soup can, U.S.A. 1960's

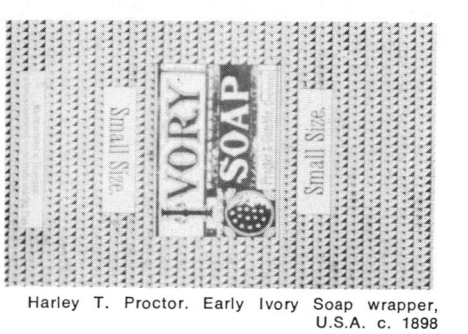

Harley T. Proctor. Early Ivory Soap wrapper, U.S.A. c. 1898

44

Columbia

Anonymous. Columbia Bicycle mark, U.S.A. c. 1888

Anonymous. Ballantine Beer mark, U.S.A. 1880

Anonymous. Colt Revolver mark, U.S.A. c. 1840.

Anonymous. Lydia E. Pinkham Company, U.S.A. 1881

Anonymous. W. Baker and Co., U.S.A. c. 1800

Anonymous. Eastman Kodak Company Cameras, U.S.A. 1888

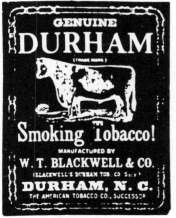

R. R. Grech. Bull Durham, U.S.A. 1866

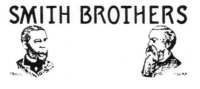

Anonymous. Smith Brothers, U.S.A. 1847

Anonymous. Victor Talking Machine, U.S.A. c. 1910

VICTORIAN PHOTOGRAPHY

John Millais. *Ophelia*, England. 1852

H. P. Robinson. *Lady of Shallot*, England. 1861

H. P. Robinson. *Fading Away*, England. 1858

Since Zuxis, an ancient Greek, painted a bunch of grapes so realistically that a dove pecked at it with his beak, Western painters have searched for ways of reproducing the physical world realistically. When the invention of the daguerreotype in 1839 and the talbotype in 1840 made it possible to reproduce the physical world by merely snapping a shutter, many painters despaired. Degas, Corot, Pissaro, Renoir and Eakins, on the other hand, made photography a useful tool. Other painters, including W. H. Hunt, John Millais and other pre-Raphaelites, ignored photography as a tool but imitated its effect in the acutely realistic details of their paintings.

While pre-Raphaelite painters were influenced by photographic technique, photographers were influenced by pre-Raphaelite subject matter. Millais' *Ophelia* was popular with the audience of 1852 because it portrayed a favorite subject, the death of a beautiful young woman, and also because Millais delineated every poppy and violet surrounding the stream-borne body with photographic realism. This realism, precisely what the Victorians admired, became even more disturbing when it was heightened by photography and applied to a similar subject by H. P. Robinson (1830–1901) in the combination print *The Lady of Shallot.*

The allegory that marked Delacroix's *Liberty Leading the People,* Cole's *The Voyage of Life* and other 19th-century paintings reached wild extremes in allegorical photography. Shortly after the Photographic Society of London was founded in 1853, Sir William Newton, a court painter, set off the debate between those who believed it wrong to tamper with a photograph and those who insisted that a photograph could be improved by artifice. The latter group, the art photographers, then developed the photographic allegory. Anecdotal and moralizing, it catered to the taste that made the opera and the novel favorite Victorian art forms.

O. G. Rejlander (1812–1875) generated interest in photographic allegory with *Two Ways of Life,* which was shown at the Manchester Art Treasures Exhibition of 1857 and later purchased by Queen Victoria. To make the picture, Rejlander photographed 25 different models in separate groups, then from some 30 separate negatives made up a final 31-by-16-inch print. The photo represents two young men led by a wise old one, "The one, calm and placid, turns toward Religion, Charity and Industry, the other rushes madly from his guide into the pleasures of the world, typified by . . . Gambling, Wine, Licentiousness . . . and ending in Suicide, Insanity, Death." The nude in the center of the composition symbolizes Repentance. Victorian in technique and subject, *Two Ways of Life* collapses as art because the inherent realism of photography undermines belief in the toga'd figures. It also collapses because coy eroticism subverts the high-toned moral. Couture's *Romans of the Decadence* and Delacroix's *Death of Sardanapalus* are more successful than *Two Ways of Life* to the degree that they were not painted with photography's unmitigated realism.

The extent to which Victorians were blind to the inappropriateness of depicting unreal subjects through the realistic medium of photography is measured in the career of Julia Margaret Cameron (1815–1879). Perhaps the greatest portrait photographer of her time, she and her contemporaries nevertheless considered *The Passing of Arthur* and similar story-illustration photos "more artistic" than her portraits. "It was a most unfortunate circumstance both for art and for photography," says photography historian Helmut Gernsheim, "that up to World War I the public, artists and art critics alike, were inclined to judge painting by photography—in its capacity for rendering detail and photography by painting—in the sphere of imaginative composition. This confusion about the aims of photography and painting led to shocking errors of taste in both media, and the good that each might have derived from the other was lost to both."

The Levantine Factor

The Picturesque esthetic accounts for the subject matter as well as the storytelling apparatus of Victorian photography. Photographers picked up the medieval themes of neo-Gothic architecture and, less often, exotic Levantine themes. Important as a source for decorative motifs in Victorian architecture and interior design, the Levant also became the setting for Mozart's *Abduction from the Seraglio,* Verdi's *Aïda* and Strauss's *Salome.* Shortly after the invasion of Egypt by Napoleon, Jean Ingres introduced the Levantine motif in *Grande Odalisque,* a nude with the headdress, feathers, and cushions of a harem girl. The Levant was also the setting for Delacroix's *Algerian Women in Their Quarters,* Ingres' *Turkish Bath,* Manet's *Olympia* and, as late as 1937, Matisse's *Odalisque.* The decoding of the Rosetta Stone in 1823 and the digging of the Suez Canal intensified public interest in the Near East. So popular had the Levant become by the 1860's that it seemed only slightly ridiculous when a New York infantry regiment, calling themselves Zouaves, marched against the Army of Northern Virginia in Turkish pantaloons.

Not surprisingly, Near Eastern themes were popular with the Victorian travel photographers. Maxime DuCamp (1822–1894) succeeded in producing an unequaled photo of Abu Simbel. Earlier, in 1856, the English landscape photographer Francis Firth (1822–1899) photographed the temples at Karnak and Luxor and the ruins of Palestine as well as Abu Simbel. His collection of views

O. J. Rejlander. *Two Ways of Life,* England. 1857

Eugene Delacroix. *Death of Sardanapalus,* France. 1827

Julia Margaret Cameron. *Passing of Arthur,* England. 1874

Maxime DuCamp. *Abu Simbel*, Egypt. 1850

Francis Firth. *Pyramids of Dashur,
Egypt.* 1858

Julia Margaret Cameron. *Mrs. Herbert Duck-
worth*, England. 1867

excited so much public interest that he went back on three more assignments, even photographing the headwaters of the Nile.

Faces from the Past

At their best, Victorian portrait photographers matched Sargent and Eakins, though not Ingres or David, in capturing the personality of their subjects. Indeed, after Cézanne, painters converted portraiture into an exercise in structural analysis and left the interpretation of character to Julia Margaret Cameron and other photographers. Among Cameron's subjects were Darwin, Ruskin, Longfellow, Carlyle, Tennyson and other eminent Victorians. Her portraits captured the power of these men and were enhanced by the powerful feelings she brought to her work. As she relates in the autobiographical *Annals of My Glass House:* "When I have had such men before my camera my whole soul had endeavored to do its duty towards them in recording faithfully the greatness of the inner as well as the features of the outer man. Thus the photograph thus taken has been almost the embodiment of a prayer."

Mrs. Cameron did not take up photography until after 40 but her home in the Isle of Wight soon became the gathering place for the British intelligentsia. All who visited sat before her camera. Every exposure took as much as five minutes, and she sometimes insisted on hundreds before she achieved the results she wanted. Mrs. Cameron used the wet-plate process invented by Scott Archer in 1851. Although faster than other processes then available, it was tedious. A glass plate had to be kept wet with collodion from the time it was placed in the camera until it was developed. If the solution dried, the plate was ruined. Mrs. Cameron deliberately used poorly ground lenses to blur the outlines of her subjects, and, unlike other photographers of the time, used less light than was naturally available in order to create dramatic shadows on the faces of her dramatic subjects.

The French portrait photographer Etienne Carjat (1828–1906) was also outstanding. Carjat's portrait of Charles Baudelaire reveals the burning intensity of the poet; paintings of Baudelaire present only the ambiguous façade of the young dandy. Gaspard-Felix Tournachon, who called himself Nadar (1820–1910), photographed Sarah Bernhardt, Theophile Gautier, Jean Baptiste Corot and other notables. His studio became a rendezvous for French artists and intellectuals.

Less dramatic but more powerful in their honesty were the portraits of two Scotsmen, Hill and Adamson. A conventional Romantic painter of ancient castles and wild landscapes, David Octavious Hill (1802–1870) would be unknown today were it not for his photographs, among the first important photographic portraits of the Victorian era. In May, 1842, a single event turned Hill into a photographer. After ten years of conflict, some 470 ministers of the Church of Scotland resigned on a matter of principle: the right of congregations to choose their own ministers instead of having them appointed by the Queen or by landed proprietors. The sacrifice of these men, who gave up their pulpits for an ideal, moved Hill. In response, he dedicated his own life to commemorating their action in a monumental painting. Only when he began to work did Hill realize the enormous difficulty of his task. Then it was suggested that Hill use the new art of photography to help him execute his portraits, and he turned to this medium as a solution. With the young chemist Robert Adamson (1821–1848), he began photographing the ministers. His enormous painting *The Signing of the Deed of Demission,* done in part from the photographs, was not finished until 23 years later. It was bought by the Free Church of Scotland in whose Edinburgh offices it still hangs.

Carjat. *Charles Baudelaire,* Paris. 1863

Today, when Hill's painting has been forgotten, his photographs evoke the haunting quality of a bygone time. The peculiarly soft and warm sepia quality of Hill's portraits is characteristic of the talbotype process. This process, patented by the amateur linguist and botanist William Henry Fox Talbot in 1841, produced a fuzzy effect because the grain of the paper on which each photo was printed interfered with the image being recorded. By contrast, the more popular daguerreotype process, introduced by Louis Jacques Daguerre two years earlier, gave a much sharper image. But the copper plate on which the image was recorded was both positive and negative, and there was no way to duplicate a print from it.

"I am fond of children, except boys," Charles Lutwidge Dodgson (1832–1898) once explained. An obsessive fondness led Dodgson (better known as Lewis Carroll, the author of *Alice in Wonderland*) to photograph dozens of Victorian nymphets and to achieve some 3,000 remarkably unstrained and charming portraits. Dodgson worked with the most primitive camera, used the wet-plate process and took exposures that lasted up to a minute and a half. Yet his photos, produced only a decade or so after the discovery of photography, are superbly natural portraits.

Nadar. *George Sand,* Paris. c. 1860

Not all Victorian portrait photographers recorded with the charm of Dodgson or honesty of Hill. The amateurs fell afoul of Picturesque sentimentality. Emile Zola, for example, hard-headed chronicler of anti-Semitism and alcoholism, produced scenes of unblushing sentimentality when he turned from pen to camera.

The popular *carte-de-visite* commercial studios repeated artificial poses unrevealing of character. The craze for *carte-de-visite* portraits started in May 1859 when Napoleon III, on his way to a campaign in Italy, is said to have halted his troops outside the photographic studio of Adolphe-Eugene Disderi

D. O. Hill and Robert Adamson.
Rev. George Gilfillan and *Dr. Samuel Brown,*
Scotland. 1843–1845

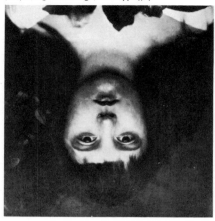

Julia Margaret Cameron. Portrait of Florence, England. 1872.

Disdéri. Lord Alfred Douglas, Paris. 1860

Emile Zola. Zola's Children, France. 1900

William Notman. Portrait of boy, Canada. c. 1860

Lewis Carroll. Alice Liddel, England. c. 1860

Adolphe Braun. Countess Castiglione, Paris. c. 1855

Anonymous. Heroes of the Goodwin Sands, England. c. 1895

Thomas Eakins. Portrait of his father-in-law, U.S.A. c. 1890

Robert Adamson. Portrait of D. O. Hill, Scotland. c. 1845

(1819–1890) to have his picture taken. Overnight Disderi became famous as Parisians flocked to his studio for portraits. But most *carte-de-visite* photos were stereotyped unless the sitter, like the irrepressible Lord Alfred Douglas, avoided conventional studio poses.

Documentary Photography

What the McCormick reaper was to proto-Functionalist product design, the documentary was to photography. Rejecting the sentimentality of the period, documentary photographers destroyed the romance of war and the charm of poverty. "It is the power of the documentary photograph to leave nothing out, to give the viewer the sense that this is truly the way it was," says historian Beaumont Newhall. And it was for this purpose—to show people back in England how it was during the Crimean War—that Roger Fenton (1819–1869) in 1855 set sail for Balaclava. Fenton's pictures were not the first news photos—these had been taken of the ruins of Hamburg after a terrible four-day fire in 1842—but they were among the first war photos. News reports of the appalling conditions of the troops had already led to the resignation of Lord Aberdeen's government. But Fenton's strangely still photos do not convey the horror that the cholera-ravaged and poorly clothed troops experienced. Perhaps, since Fenton traveled under royal patronage, he was inclined to avoid the grislier aspects of war. More likely, sheer slowness of wet-plate equipment made photographing the action of battle impossible. Unendurable heat also made the assignment difficult. Working inside the darkroom of his closed van, Fenton said, "perspiration started from every pore." By June he had to stop work at 10 in the morning. After that, "the glare was so great from the sky no one could keep his eyes more than half open."

When the American Civil War broke out, Mathew B. Brady (1823–1896) determined to record its complete visual history. Already a successful portrait photographer, he invested a fortune in outfitting and training 20 war photographers. Soon these men, with their fragile wet-plate equipment in photographic vans, were in the field. At Bull Run, Brady was almost killed, but before the brutal war was over, Alexander Gardner, Timothy O'Sullivan, William H. Jackson and his other intrepid associates had photographed battlefields, ruins, officers, enlisted men, corpses, ships and railroads. What was impossible to capture with the equipment then available was the individual human suffering that photographers of World War II would show. Although Brady's record of the war was invaluable, the U. S. Government failed to buy his collection. Even in 1871, when the Library of Congress had the opportunity to purchase it, it took no action. Three years later the U. S. War Department

Roger Fenton. *Cookhouse of the 8th Hussars, Crimea.* 1855

Alexander Gardner. *Home of a Rebel Sharpshooter,* Gettysburg, Pa. 1863

John Thomson. *Street musician from Street Life in London, England.* 1877

Jacob Riis. *Baxter Street, New York.* 1888

William Notman. *Canadian Pacific Railway,*
Glacier Park, British Columbia. c. 1889

Frances Johnson. *Students at Hampton Institute,*
Virginia. 1900

acquired 6,000 of the 8,000 negatives at an auction. Although Congress eventually paid Brady $25,000 for the copyright to these negatives, he was by then so deeply in debt that he could not get back on his feet. He died in the charity ward of a New York hospital.

Victorians neglected documenting the social conditions around them for the first decades of the photographic era. Not until the mid-seventies did John Thomson (1837–1921), working with social critic Adolph Smith, produce *Street Life in London,* the first photographic social documentation of any kind. Thomson's 36 photos show street musicians, bootblacks, locksmiths and street traders all in their usual settings. In their preface, the authors describe the function of the photos: "The unquestionable accuracy of this testimony will enable us to present true types of the London Poor and shield us from the accusation of either underrating or exaggerating individual peculiarities of appearance."

Some ten years later Jacob A. Riis (1849–1914) performed a similar service for the citizens of New York. Riis, a Dane who came to New York in 1870, suffered the hardships of so many immigrants to the New World. He knew first-hand the tenements, the all-night restaurants and the cheap lodging houses. Becoming a police reporter for *The Sun,* Riis returned to the slums to cover stories and to photograph the life there. Horrified by what he saw, he began a crusade that led to the condemnation of Mulberry Bend and other slum pockets, to housing reforms and to the building of the neighborhood house that bears his name. Unfortunately, because of inadequate reproduction techniques, most of Riis's photos in his reports for *The Sun* as well as in his book, *How the Other Half Lives,* were printed as line drawings. The result was that Riis's photos almost passed into oblivion. Not until 1947, when photographer Alexander Alland made enlargements from the original negatives at the Museum of the City of New York, did the public become aware of the moving visual record Riis left.

The Canadian portrait photographer William Notman left an invaluable legacy of thousands of photos recording every aspect of Canadian life between 1850 and World War I. Frances B. Johnson, another early documentary photographer, left carefully posed but moving photos of Hampton Institute, alma mater of Booker T. Washington and other black leaders.

The Snapshot

Photography appealed to the Victorian's love of gadgetry and to his respect for technological achievement. Even before the gates of the Crystal Palace opened, the camera was a serious scientific instrument. By that date photographers had taken the first micrograph (the eye of a fly), the first travel photos (Smyrna and Malta), the first ethnological photos (tribes in Brazil) and the first astronomical photos (of the sun and the moon). It was the amateur photographer who, demanding simplified picture-taking equipment, encouraged innovations in the technology of photography. The greatest stimulus to amateur photography occurred in August, 1888, when George Eastman introduced the Kodak camera. It cost $25, including leather case, and was the last word in simplicity and technology. By 1891 Eastman had sold 90,000 cameras and even Edgar Degas and George Bernard Shaw had become amateur photographers.

Capturing Motion

Movement fascinated Victorians. Swivel chairs, hammocks, roller skates and bicycles kept them in perpetual motion. It is not surprising that they exploited the camera both to create motion and to stop motion. In 1832 experimenters utilized a phenomenon called persistence of vision—with a dish-like device depicting the same figure in slightly varying positions, they created the illusion of motion. This led, with the improvement of the camera and roll film system, to moving pictures—a new art form combining the graphic qualities of painting with the dramatic qualities of theater.

Eadweard Muybridge (1830–1904), an Englishman living in the United States, pioneered the stopping of motion on film. He used many different rigs, among them a single bank of cameras whose shutters were tripped by the movement of the subject. He also used banks of cameras in different positions to record the movement of a subject from three positions at the same moment. His remarkable photos showed for the first time how a horse gallops and how a person walks, and aided such painters as Thomas Eakins as well as doctors working with crippled patients.

J. E. Marey (1830–1904), a French physiologist interested in discovering the secret of how birds fly, used a portable photographic gun rather than Muybridge's cumbersome bank of cameras to photograph his elusive subjects. The effect, similar to that of strobe photography, was recreated by Marcel Duchamp in *Nude Descending a Staircase* and by Giacomo Balla in *Dog on a Leash*. These paintings, which drew upon the stop-motion images of scientific strobe photography, marked a beginning for Modern painting.

Eadweard Muybridge. *Study of horses walking.* U.S.A. 1880

E. J. Marey. *Study of man jumping,* Paris. 1885

Giacomo Balla. *Dynamism of a Dog on Leash,* Italy. 1912

ART NOUVEAU

The Misunderstood Revolution

Louis Sullivan. Ironwork decoration.
Schlessinger-Meyer Department Store, Chicago.
1903–1904

Anonymous. Shoe, France. 1902

Victor Horta. Van Eetvelde house, Brussels. 1895

Peter Behrens. Electric tea kettles, Germany, 1912

Dozens of Victorian architects had found in the neo-Gothic Houses of Parliament a model for Picturesque homes and public buildings. The Crystal Palace, on the other hand, had remained a stylistic exception. During the Art Nouveau decades of 1880–1910, designers cultivated biomorphic artifacts, such as the sunflower-shaped lamps designed by the Belgian architect Victor Horta for the van Eetvelde house. Even footwear designers, appliquéing whiplash patterns onto women's shoes, worked in the Curvilinear mode. Geometric forms, such as those favored by the German industrial designer Peter Behrens, were popular only among German, Viennese and Scotch designers. While the whiplash line of Curvilinear Art Nouveau reiterated the concave-convex line of Victorian Picturesque, the less widespread Rectilinear Art Nouveau introduced geometric forms that would dominate style in the 20th century.

Factory technology had made possible the construction of the Crystal Palace, and its very look seemed to express the new age of steam-driven machinery. After Edison invented the incandescent light in 1879, electricity provided a new source for power, and Art Nouveau's whiplash line, suggesting a pulsing electric wave, dominated style in the following decade.

In what sense was Art Nouveau revolutionary? Most important, it offered a new vocabulary of form, line and color. Outline, as in the candelabrum (page 65) by van de Velde, rather than surface decoration, as in Angell's flagons (page 33), provides visual interest. Pattern dominates subject, Symbol replaces anecdote.

Art Nouveau was also revolutionary in adopting a Symbolist esthetic of form and pattern. Where Victorian designers had revived elements of Egyptian, Gothic and other historical styles to induce specific associations in the viewer, Art Nouveau designers introduced peacocks, lilies, swans, and other symbols to stand for specific ideas.

Lastly, Art Nouveau was revolutionary in embracing an esthetic in which the function of an object influenced its form. In the Victorian period not even locomotives or machine tools had been designed to look functional—though often they were superbly so. In the Art Nouveau period even housewares began to be functional—and they looked it.

In what sense was Art Nouveau misunderstood? First, it was not a short-lived "decorative disease," as artist Walter Crane called it. It was an authentic stage of the Modern style, and it spanned more than thirty years. As early as 1878 the Catalonian architect Antonio Gaudí had twisted Curvilinear forms into the ironwork of the Casa Vicens, and as late as 1911 Gustav Klimt, a Viennese painter, had contained intricate patterns within the unbroken outline of the two figures in his Stoclet House mural (page 71). Second, it did not originate in France, as the English thought when they affixed the label, but in England as the French thought. Finally, Art Nouveau was not insignificant. It destroyed the revivalist-associative Picturesque esthetic and saw the first significant expression of a sustained preference, on the part of a growing number of influential designers, for the geometric forms and straight or angular lines which were to overshadow all of 20th-century design.

The whiplash, the most popular Curvilinear motif of the Art Nouveau period, did not meet with unqualified approval. Because of it, the offended Belgians called Art Nouveau *Paling stil* (eel style), the Germans, *Schnorkelstil* (noodle style) and *Bandwurmstil* (tapeworm style). These disparaging terms were not misplaced. Art Nouveau's characteristic biomorphic form was, indeed, noodle-like. Contrasted against the Curvilinear biomorphic forms of the Art Nouveau period was a strong and vital Rectilinear mode, exemplified by the work of Charles Rennie Mackintosh in Glasgow and Joseph Hoffman in Vienna.

Alien Roots

The seemingly new forms of Art Nouveau actually had ancient precedent in *The Book of Kells* and other illuminated Celtic manuscripts. Caught up in the turn-of-the-century revival of Irish and Scottish culture, designers borrowed from these manuscripts interlace patterns, abstract animal forms, ribbonlike lines, coiled spirals and whiplash curves. William Butler Yeats wrote of "old Eire and the ancient ways." Mackintosh, painting Celt-derived ribbon patterns into his posters, also appealed to national pride.

Victor Horta. Iron work, Horta House, Brussels. 1890

If some of what seems strange in Art Nouveau grows from these Celtic roots, much of the rest springs from the Japanese print. As the Celtic manuscript was a source for Rectilinear Art Nouveau, so the Japanese print was a source for Curvilinear Art Nouveau. James MacNeil Whistler was among the first to collect Japanese prints. He showed them to designers, who imitated their sophisticated handling of negative space, their emphasis of line and outline and their flattening of surfaces.

Less alien was the influence of William Morris, the designer, and William Blake, the British poet, printer and philosopher. Blake's *Songs of Innocence*, in which poems were illustrated with wood cuts, taught designers to integrate words and pictures on a page. His androgynous figures were transformed into epicine boys by Aubrey Beardsley, into ethereal ladies by Mackintosh. William Morris's idea of a guild of craftsmen encouraged Arthur H. Mackmurdo to found the Century Guild and Walter Crane the Art Workers Guild. These younger men shared Morris's belief in the indivisible unity of the arts but not his rejection of the machine and mass production.

Antonio Gaudi. Casa Güell, Barcelona. 1878

The Symbolist Esthetic

Not only did Symbolist poets provide symbols for Art Nouveau designers, they also provided theory—most important, that the barriers that separate one art from another should be torn down. It was this idea that led Claude Debussy to set to music Mallarmé's *L'Après-midi d'un faune,* Richard Strauss to convert Wilde's *Salome* to an opera and Schönberg to use Art Nouveau poems in *Pierrot Lunaire.* As for designers, no period produced so many who worked in more than one discipline: Beardsley, Rossetti and Morris were poets as well as artists. Van de Velde not only designed tapestries and furniture but also wrote on design theory, while Mackintosh designed furniture, posters and light fixtures as well as buildings. The symbols introduced by Yeats, Mallarmé and Verlaine were not the only ones to influence design. The lily, having first appeared in the pre-Raphaelite paintings of Dante Gabriel Rossetti, became the heraldic emblem of Art Nouveau. The iris, the poppy and the tulip also figured importantly. Swans were another favorite symbol, popularized by Tchaikovsky's *Swan Lake* and by Wagner's *Lohengrin.* Hair, more incarnation than symbol of the feminine, coiled down the murals of Mackintosh, twisted through the illustrations of Beardsley and filled the mosaics of Gustav Klimt.

While most Art Nouveau designers tied their work to the idealistic socialism of Morris, some preferred the hot-house exoticism of Oscar Wilde. The "decadent" aspect of Art Nouveau design, its extremes of form and its overrefinement, paralleled the literary experiments of Wilde, Huysmans and other writers. "The most representative literature of the day," the English writer Arthur Symons said in 1892, "is certainly not classic. It is no doubt a decadence; it has all the qualities that mark the end of great periods . . . an intense self-consciousness, a restless curiosity in research, and oversubtilizing refinement upon refinement, a spiritual and moral perversity. If what we call the classic is indeed the supreme art—with its qualities of perfect simplicity, perfect sanity, perfect proportion—then this representative literature of today, interesting, beautiful, novel as it is, is really a new and beautiful and interesting disease." The same was said about Art Nouveau design. Nevertheless, both "decadent" and socialist designers wished to synthesize the arts. Their difference was in taste rather than technique, in content rather than style: Aubrey Beardsley's *Yellow Book,* the most sophisticated magazine of the period, was different in spirit but not style from Mackmurdo's earnest publication, *The Hobby Horse.*

Aubrey Beardsley. *Yellow Book,* England. 1890

Arthur Mackmurdo. *Hobby Horse,* England. 1886

ART NOUVEAU GRAPHICS

Nowhere was the shift from the Victorian to the Art Nouveau stage of the Modern style more striking than in graphic design. The Victorian poster had been a busy jumble of illustration and typography. The Art Nouveau poster was boldly simple. White space became a positive design element, and designers restricted pattern to specific areas. The realistic figure, so much a part of the storytelling apparatus in Victorian design, evolved into an abstraction. From Japanese prints Art Nouveau designers learned what their Victorian predecessors had not known—how to flatten surfaces and to utilize negative space.

In the title page for *Wren's City Churches* (1883) Arthur Heygate Mackmurdo (1851–1942) designed one of the earliest woodcuts of the Art Nouveau period. With its attenuated cranes and semi-abstract thistles, it departed sharply from Victorian precedent. Though he was a prophet of the graphic look most closely associated with the Art Nouveau period, Mackmurdo gave up design and architecture about 1900 and retired to study economics in Essex where he lived until his death. His abrupt and total withdrawal from the design arts parallels the disaffectation of Victor Horta, a Belgian architect, and Ernst Ludwig Kirchner, a German painter, with some of their early Art Nouveau work. Kirchner even refused to acknowledge his own woodcuts.

The New Look in Typography

Eugene Grasset (1841–1917), a Swiss-born French illustrator, designed the first Art Nouveau type face in 1820. Only a subtle departure from previous faces, Grasset's was closely related to Old Style types in that it did not strongly contrast thick and thin lines.

Otto Eckmann (1865–1902), a German artist, followed Grasset's work with graphic experiments for the German Art Nouveau magazines, *Pan* and *Jugend.* As a result of this work, he was commissioned to design a type face in the Art Nouveau style. Eckmann's face, called Fette Eckmann, is based on the Roman alphabet, but the letters, no longer regularly curved and straight-lined, resemble the serpentine curves of Beardsley and van de Velde. Areas of the "A," "D" and "P" that are normally closed have been opened to connect them with the white space of the page and to increase the interplay of positive and negative space. The versatile Henri van de Velde also experimented with letter forms, transforming them into non-objective—and non-readable—but decorative arabesques. Peter Behrens, on the other hand, with catalogs for AEG (page 60), strengthened the Rectilinear mode of Art Nouveau.

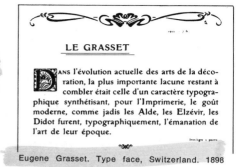

LE GRASSET

ANS l'évolution actuelle des arts de la décoration, la plus importante lacune restant à combler était celle d'un caractère typographique synthétisant, pour l'Imprimerie, le goût moderne, comme jadis les Alde, les Elzévir, les Didot furent, typographiquement, l'émanation de l'art de leur époque.

Eugene Grasset. Type face, Switzerland. 1898

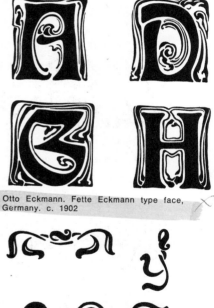

Otto Eckmann. Fette Eckmann type face, Germany. c. 1902

Henri van de Velde. Lettering, Belgium. 1893

The New Look in Posters

Jules Cheret (1836–1932), a French package designer, had been the first to introduce Art Nouveau elements to the poster, and, in retrospect, it is not surprising that van de Velde, in an essay demanding a new kind of art, should have cited Cheret's posters as a source of inspiration. Cheret, with strong colors, simple outlines and bold lettering, helped formulate the characteristic look of the Art Nouveau poster. Not always of first quality themselves, his posters were an important influence on Bonnard and van de Velde.

Bonnard introduced Henri de Toulouse-Lautrec (1864–1901) to the art of poster making in 1891. With talent too large for the stylistic confines of Art Nouveau, Toulouse-Lautrec exploited its mannerisms to bring the poster to its highest development. Often restricting himself to a single dramatic silhouette drawn with the fewest possible lines, he simplified the poster. He drew his figures from unusual viewpoints in order to achieve the most powerful combination of shapes and capped off the dramatic effect with bold, freely drawn lettering. One of the first serious artists to experiment with color lithography, Toulouse-Lautrec mastered the tedious process of executing a separate lithographic stone for each color. Less significant as a painter—often paintings were mere starting points for his lithographs—he became one of the greatest masters of color lithography. For subjects he chose the prostitutes, alcoholics and singers of Montmartre, and he presented them without sentimentality or

Alfons Mucha. *Salon des Cent*, France. 1896

Peter Behrens. Catalog cover, Germany. 1908

Arthur Mackmurdo. *Wren's City Churches*, England, 1883

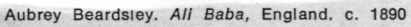

Aubrey Beardsley. *Ali Baba*, England. c. 1890

vulgarity. "Everywhere and always ugliness has its beautiful aspects," he said to the dance-hall chanteuse Yvette Guilbert. "It is thrilling to discover them where nobody else had noticed them."

Aubrey Vincent Beardsley (1872–1898) combined an elegant attenuated line with a sickly eroticism entirely different from Toulouse-Lautrec's harsh realism. Toulouse-Lautrec had chosen to document life in the bordellos of Paris. Beardsley chose to illustrate Alexander Pope's *The Rape of the Lock*. Toulouse-Lautrec pressed line into biting caricature of Yvette Guilbert or La Goulue. In his treatment of clothing and especially of hair, Beardsley allowed line to become self-preoccupied. The result was that Toulouse-Lautrec's portraits revealed the inner life of the subject whereas Beardsley, avoiding encounters with real people, concealed his message behind symbols. Beardsley drew pictures as though his first commandment were Oscar Wilde's statement: "All art is at once surface and symbol. Those who go beneath the surface do so at their peril. Those who read the symbol do so at their peril."

Of Beardsley's work art historian Robert Schmutzler has said: "Intellectual art of this kind expresses neither warmth nor sentiment, but is endowed with elegance and an infernal and disturbing grace." Beardsley became art editor of the *Yellow Book* at 22, and the next year joined *The Savoy*. By then he had become, along with Toulouse-Lautrec, the most significant graphic designer of the Art Nouveau period. He died at 26.

Scores of other designers were influenced by these masters. Alfons Maria

Pierre Bonnard. *La Revue Blanche*, France. 1894

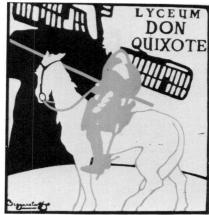

Beggarstaff brothers. *Don Quixote*, Engand. 1895

Henri de Toulouse-Lautrec. *Moulin Rouge*, France. 1893

Jules Cheret. *Palais de Glace*, Paris. 1896

P. H. Emerson. *Ricking the Reed.* 1886

Henri Lartigue. *Paris Boulevard,* Paris. c. 1910

Anonymous. *Lawn party,* England. c. 1890

John Thomson, *Hong Kong Harbor,* Hong Kong. c. 1890

Eugene Atget, *Shop window.* Paris. 1910

Anonymous. *Mary Garden,* U.S.A. c. 1910

Anonymous. *Lady with parasol,* U.S.A. c. 1900

Frederick Hillyer. *Mrs. William Morris,* England. c. 1885

O. Marotz. *Portrait of a Farmer,* Vienna. 1897

Mucha (1860–1939), a Czech painter, executed posters of Sarah Bernhardt that made him, as well as the actress, famous. From his studio in Chicago, designer Will Bradley won international recognition for his art direction of *Century* magazine and of *The Chapbook*. He later worked for American Type Founders, where he set fashion in typography for decades. The Beggarstaff brothers, actually James Pryde and William Nicholson, established high standards for English graphic design during the same period.

ART NOUVEAU PHOTOGRAPHY

Like other design media, turn-of-the-century photography reflected an Art Nouveau influence. While the early photographs of Edward Steichen possess something of the look, the work of a bookseller and amateur photographer, Frederick H. Evans (1853–1943), best expresses it. Evans's greatest photos were of architecture, especially the medieval cathedrals of England. His dramatic use of light and shadow and his emphasis on form to evoke emotion placed him within the framework. Evans believed the photographer could better the painter in portraiture, and his unforgettable photo of Beardsley supports him. The father of architectural photography, Evans was prominent in photographic circles from 1895 until the 1930's. But his work had almost been forgotten until it was exhibited by Beaumont Newhall at George Eastman House in 1964.

P. H. Emerson (1856–1936), a Suffolk County English doctor and amateur photographer, rejected art photography as it had been practiced by the Victorians. At 26, after spending his boyhood in Massachusetts and earning a medical degree from Cambridge, he joined the Royal Photographic Society, whose exhibitions of combination prints, sentimentalized photos of peasant life and imitation paintings enraged him. Abandoning his career as a doctor, Emerson brought nature photography to new heights. Emerson used the dry-plate process invented by another English doctor, Richard Leach Maddox, in 1871. This process made commercial manufacture of plates possible and freed Emerson and others from the nuisance of making their own. Between 1866 and 1895 Emerson published seven picture books on East Anglian peasant and fisherfolk life.

In 1889 he published *Naturalistic Photography,* an idiosyncratic work that set forth a new concept of pictorial photography and backed up the virtues of differential focusing with scientific data. It also dismissed lovers of Michelangelo as "frugivorous apes." Emerson urged simplicity of means and the avoidance of props, artificial costumes or poses. He condemned retouching as a means of "perverting the truth of the picture." Above all, he proclaimed

Frederick Evans. *Wells Cathedral,* England. 1903

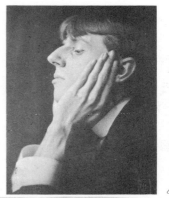

Frederick Evans. *Aubrey Beardsley,* England. c. 1894

P. H. Emerson. *Pond in Winter,* England. 1888

P. H. Emerson. *Gunner Working up to Fowl,*
England. 1886

Edward Steichen. *Steeplechase Day,* Paris. 1905

Robert Demachy, *Ballerina,* U.S.A. c. 1900

"pure photography" as a fine art. True to his mercurial nature, Emerson recanted the belief in photography as fine art two years later with *The Death of Naturalistic Photography.* His own photos, though sometimes posed and picturesque in studied casualness of composition, possess a soft stillness akin to impressionist painting.

Emerson proselytized for photography as an art peculiar to itself during the same time that Robert Demachy, George Davidson and Heinrich Kuhn, who led the art photography movement in Austria, were becoming entranced with the dream of making photographs into imitation paintings. To help them, there were a number of new technical processes.

Eugene Atget (1856–1927) documented the monuments, streets and shopwindows of Paris. He earned his living by selling these photos to painters who used them as studies. Ironically, Atget's photos are more admired today than the paintings for which they served as studies. Although Atget's intention was to document, he brought to his work a painter's concern for perspective and biaxial symmetry.

The bromoil process, introduced by E. J. Wall and C. Welborne Piper in 1907, produced a gelatine relief print that would take up oil pigment of any color applied with a brush. The oil-pigment process, introduced by G. E. H. Rawlins in 1904, produced a gelatine relief with raised highlights. The picture was made by dabbing oil pigment on the moist print with a brush. The gelatine accepted or rejected the pigment according to the degree to which the light action had taken place on the bichromated gelatine. The gum-print process, introduced in 1894 and popularized by Robert Demachy the following year, required the coating of sized paper with rubber cement, potassium bichromate and watercolor pigment. The photographer controlled his picture by modifying the coating and washing process. By choosing different types of paper and pigment colors, he could create variations of the same picture.

Demachy not only used the gum-printing process but, by exposing the negative to coarse canvas, actually imitated the texture of canvas in his prints. Using ballet girls as the subject of one photo, Demachy imitated the subject, as well as the effect, of Degas's ballerina paintings.

While the photographs of Demachy retain considerable charm, the work of contemporaries who actually reconstituted paintings by Gainsborough, Frans Hals and other masters is difficult to accept today as more than a misguided effort by experimenters unaware of the ways in which photography differs from painting.

ART NOUVEAU PRODUCT DESIGN

Fired by the sermons of Ruskin and Morris, many artists gave up careers as painters to become what would later be designated industrial designers. Aside from Louis Comfort Tiffany and a few others, Art Nouveau designers welcomed machine technology and recognized mass production as an opportunity to spread their work on a scale never before possible.

Henri van de Velde (1863–1957), who began as a painter, ended by defining a role for the industrial designer. In *Die Renaissance in Modernen Kunstgewerbe* (1901) he wrote of the designer's relation to machine production and provided the philosophical groundwork for the first generation of industrial designers.

In its breadth, his own career foreshadowed that of the industrial designer. Van de Velde's best designs were for furniture and posters, but he also designed housewares and even clothes for his wife. Van de Velde wove elegant arabesques into script lettering (page 59) and his silver candelabrum (right), but his severe, unornamented Rectilinear chairs point toward the Functionalist mode of the Modern style.

Germany: Birthplace of Industrial Design

Even before 1900, Germany had raised industrial design standards to spur trade, and by 1907 the *Deutscher Werkbund* had been founded to promote industrial design. With its establishment, the role of the industrial designer was officially recognized by German industry. Lacking the British prejudice against machine-made goods, German manufacturers and consumers were less disposed than the British to compare them to supposedly superior hand-made goods. With Germany's keen enthusiasm for machine production, it is not surprising that Rectilinear Art Nouveau, whose forms are related to machine forms, was cultivated by German designers.

The predilection for geometric forms and undecorated surfaces is obvious in the pioneering industrial designs of Peter Behrens (1868–1940). For AEG Behrens designed style-setting electrical appliances (page 56) as well as buildings, exhibitions and catalogs (page 60). This dramatized the industrial designer's role in industry and the need for a spectrum of corporate design services directed by one man. Walter Gropius, Mies van der Rohe and Le Corbusier, the three giants of 20th-century design, all studied with the gifted Behrens.

Just as steam brought with it the sidewheeler and iron horse, so electricity generated an array of new products and, with them, new design problems.

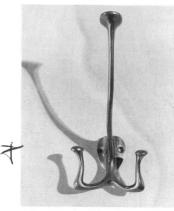

Richard Reimerschmid. Coathook, Germany. 1906

Henri van de Velde. Candelabrum, Belgium. c. 1902

Louis Tiffany. Table Lamp, U.S.A. c. 1900

Richard Reimerschmid. Lamp, Germany. 1899

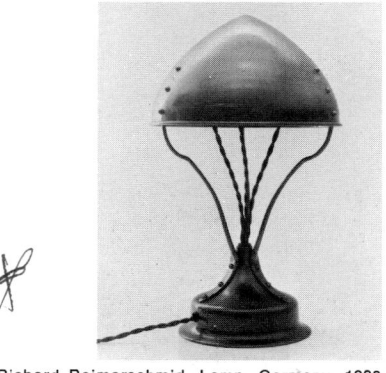

Richard Reimerschmid. Lamp, Germany. 1908

Especially baffling was the problem of designing an electric lamp. Tiffany, Guimard and Horta fashioned lamps into trees and tulips. The German designer Richard Reimerschmid (1868–1957) took a more practical approach by searching for a solution in terms of function. Although his lamp of 1899 is a tortured daffodil, the one of 1908 replaces all organic plant forms with geometric ones that interfere neither with how the lamp is manufactured nor how it will be used. With the exception of the daffodil lamp, Reimerschmid's earlier work, though Curvilinear, is clearly designed in terms of function.

Reimerschmid's artfully wrought coathook is a functioning coathook as well as a delightful piece of sculpture. But while emphasizing form rather than surface decoration, this coathook echoes the arabesques of van de Velde's candelabrum. Reimerschmid's delicately scaled silver flatware is free of ornament. The addition of a cutting edge to the cake fork and a grip handle to the dinner knife is, like later Bauhaus design, based on analysis of the function of each implement.

More concerned with appearance than function, French Art Nouveau designers developed sensuous forms from their 18th-century rococo heritage. The Paris Metro street furniture of Hector Guimard (1867–1947) gave Paris its distinctive look at the turn of the century. Guimard's coiling kiosks and blossomlike light fixtures so impressed the French that they renamed Art Nouveau *style de bouche de Metro*—though Guimard himself preferred the term *style Guimard*. S. Bing, the Belgian entrepreneur, was aware that technological innovation would require designers to develop new forms. "Amidst this universal upheaval of scientific discoveries," said Bing of the period into which Art Nouveau was born, "the decoration of the day continued to be copied from what was in vogue in previous centuries." To tug style into step with technology, Bing opened a Paris shop in 1890 which displayed furniture by Henri van de Velde, posters by Aubrey Beardsley and Charles Rennie Mackintosh, glass by Louis Comfort Tiffany and Emile Gallé, paintings by Pierre Bonnard, Henri de Toulouse-Lautrec and Edouard Vuillard, sculpture by Auguste Rodin. Bing named the shop *L'Art Nouveau,* then publicized both the name and the new look throughout Europe.

Decline of the Handcraft Tradition

Art Nouveau never decorated an American city as it had Paris, but it did penetrate thousands of American homes in the tree-shaped lamps, iridescent glass bowls and stained glass windows of Louis Comfort Tiffany (1849–1933). Instead of joining the family business, Tiffany studied painting with George Innes. He later studied the chemistry of glass and, with his friend the painter John

La Farge, worked in the glass factories of Brooklyn. By 1876 he had produced his first ornamental opalescent-glass windows; a few years later he applied for patents on the metallic, iridescent "favrile" glass for which he became famous.

His early work shows the neo-Romanesque influence of Richardson and of Near and Far Eastern art, but Tiffany soon developed an original look. Too literal an imitation of nature to be functional, and too personal to be revivalist, this look cannot be separated from Tiffany's complicated handcraft technique, a process of simultaneously blowing the glass and exposing it to chemicals and fumes of molten metals. Unlike Emile Gallé, the French "art glass" designer who cut shapes from layers of colored glass, Tiffany ran the molten glass of different colors together to achieve abstract, exotic patterns.

Once his work had aroused European interest, Tiffany executed windows designed by Bonnard, Vuillard and Toulouse-Lautrec. He also decorated part of the White House, a chapel for the World Columbian Exposition and a flamboyant mosaic-glass curtain for the National Theatre in Mexico. Tiffany later designed jewelry and built and furnished Laurelton Hall, his home in Oyster Bay, Long Island.

Richard Reimerschmid. Flatware, Germany. 1900

Victor Horta. Lamp for Solvay House, Brussels. 1895–1900

Hector Guimard. Metro sign, Paris. c. 1900

ART NOUVEAU INTERIOR DESIGN

The Art Nouveau interior differed from the Victorian interior in look and purpose. The decorator of the Milligan house (page 30) had stuffed its parlor with knickknacks, and later Victorian decorators would shade their parlors in gloom. By contrast, Victor Horta increased the size of the Solvay House windows, used a skylight in the van Eetvelde House and electric lights in the Tassel—all in order to flood his interiors with light. The Art Nouveau chair also contrasted with its Victorian counterpart. It was lighter, and often, as in the case of those designed by the German Michael Thonet, it depended for interest on sculptural form rather than on realistically carved flowers and fruit. In short, the new interior was to be bright, light, simple and spare. Its new purpose was to function with all the economy of a ship's cabin.

The Mauve Decade

Red-and-gold, the opulent color scheme found in the Milligan house and other fashionable Victorian homes, was replaced by Art Nouveau designers with sophisticated combinations of gray, pink, apple green and olive. Most popular among the new pastels was mauve—a shade that would not have been

Victor Horta. Tassel House, interior, Brussels. 1892–1893

Michael Thonet. Vienna café chair, Germany. 1859

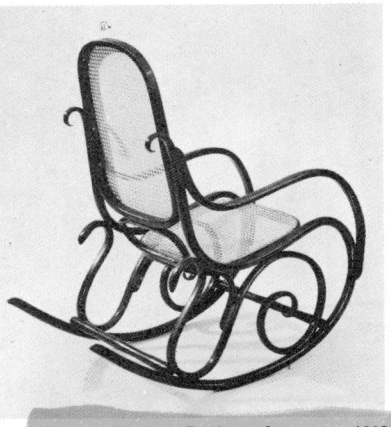

Michael Thonet. Rocker, Germany. 1860

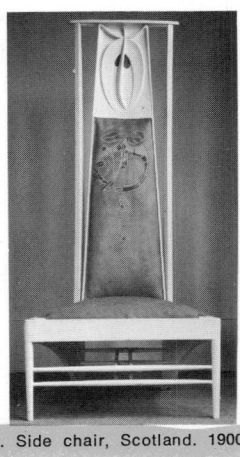

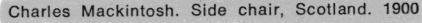

Charles Mackintosh. Side chair, Scotland. 1900

available without modern technology. The English chemist William Perkin, who synthesized aniline purple in 1856, gave the public its first commercial synthetic dye in a shade that, until then, had been reserved for kings. Ironically, the British public failed to accept aniline purple until the last decade of the century, after Parisian style-setters had dubbed it "mauve."

Art Nouveau design was peculiarly two-dimensional. This quality, so apparent in Gustav Klimt's mosaics, Tiffany's stained glass windows and Mackintosh's wall stencils, was, of course, more appropriate for interior design than for architecture. Even the slender, flat-backed chairs of Mackintosh had a peculiarly two-dimensional quality. And Horta, perhaps the most characteristic Art Nouveau architect, was more successful when designing, for example, the wall and floor surfaces for the Tassel house than when attacking three-dimensional problems. For the Tassel house he reiterated the richly biomorphic pattern of the wall and ceiling on the tile floor, and translated it into the light fixtures, cast-iron columns and wrought-iron banister. Horta's synthesis of all the elements in the Tassel house interior reflects the Art Nouveau dictum that all the arts should be synthesized. His use of iron for this domestic interior was to have the same liberating effect as Mies's use of steel for the Barcelona chair, both materials having had only industrial applications previously.

Richard Reimerschmid. Side chair, Germany. 1899

Thonet: Precursor of Curvilinear Art Nouveau

The most important Curvilinear Art Nouveau chairs were the rocker and side chair of Michael Thonet (1796–1871). Though introduced some twenty years before the Art Nouveau movement gained real momentum, their remarkable linear quality, along with their daringly modern means of production, stamps this furniture as Art Nouveau. For the Vienna café chair Thonet designed a form so simple, graceful and spare that it has not aged since it appeared in 1859. For the rocker he designed a line related both to the Picturesque Victorian line and the whiplash Art Nouveau line. It is his emphasis on form rather than surface decoration that places the chair more satisfactorily within the Art Nouveau than the Victorian framework.

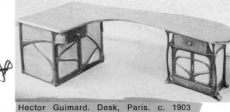

Hector Guimard. Desk, Paris. c. 1903

Thonet began to use machine techniques for the mass production of chairs in 1830 when he subjected glue-saturated veneer strips to heat and then molded them into chairs. He found that laminated-wood rods, steamed and bent, would not crack like straight-grained wood carved into the same sort of shapes. This discovery preceded Belter's patented technique (page 31) of the 1850's and, of course, Alvar Aalto's of the 1930's (page 88). The value of Thonet's technique was that untrained workmen could produce furniture in

Henri van de Velde. Desk, Belgium. 1897

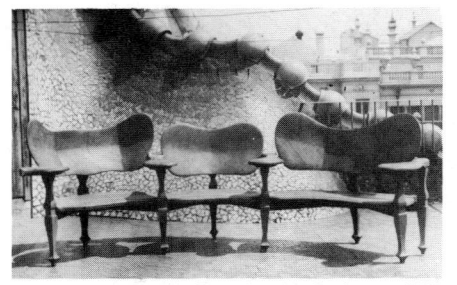

Antonio Gaudi. Curved sofa, Spain. c. 1905

Antonio Gaudi. Casa Batllo, Barcelona.
1904–1906

Charles Mackintosh. Library, Glasgow School
of Art, Glasgow. 1907–1909

assembly-line fashion. Thonet located factories near the beechwood forests that supplied his wood and developed a worldwide organization that had sold more than 50 million Vienna chairs before World War II, and continues to sell some 50,000 a year.

Van de Velde, like Horta, planned highly unified interiors that were part of a single, all-encompassing look. He not only designed his wife's dress to complement his furnishings, but, according to Toulouse-Lautrec—who visited his home—chose food to harmonize in color with the table setting. When he later achieved the same unified effect in rooms designed for Bing's shop, the journalist Edmond de Goncourt ridiculed their "yachting style." But, insofar as every item was designed for function, the term was more flattering and fitting than de Goncourt had intended.

Similar in shape to van de Velde's desk is one of asymmetrical form designed by Guimard. But this, like Guimard's street furniture for the Metro (page 67), crawls with plantlike decoration. Unlike van de Velde's "yachting-style" interiors, Guimard's interiors subordinate function to decoration.

The Germans Richard Reimerschmid and Peter Behrens brought the same simplicity to furniture design that they had brought to product design. Reimerschmid's side chair for the Dresden Exhibition of 1899 utilized the same functionalist principles that would inform Bauhaus design. Although the chair's seat is traditional, it has an unconventional curving back that the rear legs slant upward to support. The Museum of Modern Art has compared the purity and originality of this chair to Mies's cantilevered tubular steel chair (page 88) and Eames's molded plywood chair.

Gaudi's Marine Interiors

The walls of the Casa Batlló, like those of a sand castle, appear to be eroded by lapping water. They undulate as if seen through a column of water. The Casa Batlló seems stranger to foreigners than to Spaniards, who recognize its debt to Spanish Baroque. The irregular pattern around the interior doors and the sculpted chairs are entirely the product of Gaudí's Surrealist fantasy. Bizarre and playful in mood, Gaudí's hand-made chair, like this interior, is unrelated to an industrialized society. It is precisely Gaudí's refusal to acknowledge the machine that, in a machine-dominated age, gives his chairs and interiors their compelling attraction.

Mackintosh's Rectilinear Interiors

Thonet's chairs pioneered Art Nouveau's Curvilinear mode. Charles Rennie Mackintosh's, though custom-made only, helped define Rectilinear Art Nouveau. Geometric form, thin, flat planes and smooth surfaces are emphasized. Mackintosh made his chairs distinctive by painting them white and decorating them with trefoils, ovals and semi-abstract flower motifs. These unique decorations were the work of his wife, Margaret, and her sister, Frances, who had married Mackintosh's partner. Mackintosh set his dramatically Rectilinear tables and chairs into white-walled interiors, then stenciled his wife's decorations onto chair backs and into wall friezes. In his library for the Glasgow School of Art, Mackintosh exploits simple wooden beams with the sophistication of a Japanese architect. Having apparently exhausted the rich vein of his ideas in the effort to forge a new style, Mackintosh moved, after 1909, to Port Vendres, France, where he painted watercolors for many years.

Beyond Glasgow, Rectilinear Art Nouveau flourished in Berlin and Vienna. Like Mackintosh, the Viennese architect Josef Hoffman (1870–1955) worked in cubes and rectangles, but where Mackintosh had used the patterns created by his wife and sister-in-law for decorative relief, Hoffman turned to the Byzantine-derived mosaics of Gustav Klimt, an Austrian painter. For the dining-room of Hoffmann's Palais Stoclet, Klimt designed a mosaic whose rich surface of glass, semi-precious stones, white marble and enamel echoes the splendors of Ravenna. His portraits of Viennese *femmes fatales* combine representation with precociously abstract geometric ornament in a way that would not be attempted again until the 1960's.

Josef Hoffmann. B. H. Villa, Vienna. c. 1904

Gustav Klimt. *Frau Adele Bloch-Bauer*, Vienna. 1907

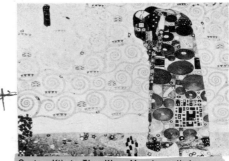

Gustav Klimt. *The Kiss*. Mosaic wall for Palais Stoclet, Brussels. 1905–1911

ART NOUVEAU ARCHITECTURE

Few major turn-of-the-century architects worked exclusively in the Rectilinear or Curvilinear mode. Louis Sullivan, the American, reflects the Curvilinear mode of Art Nouveau in naturalistic decorative details, and Antonio Gaudi, the Spaniard, in biomorphic forms, but other aspects of their work are Rectilinear. Mackintosh, Hoffman and Adolf Loos, another Viennese architect, showed a Rectilinear preference for untextured and unpapered interior walls. But Hoffmann and Mackintosh, if not Loos, favored Curvilinear decorative details. Horta (1861–1947), the architect most frequently associated with Art Nouveau, developed a unique Art Nouveau vocabulary for his own house and for the Solvay House, but worked in a different vein when he came to design the Maison du Peuple, headquarters for the Belgian Socialist Party.

Victor Horta. Horta house, Brussels. 1898

He exhibits mastery of decorative detail in the skillfully planned doorway of the Solvay House. The gracefully drooping glass panels, set off by two teardrop-shaped panels, contrast surprisingly with the ground floor windows, whose utter lack of ornament forecasts his design for the Maison du Peuple. These windows, like those in the upper stories, have been enlarged almost to the point of converting the façade into a glass curtain-wall in order to allow for the entry of maximum sunlight. The exterior of Horta's own house is remarkable primarily for its ironwork balconies.

In the Maison du Peuple, his largest building, Horta treats the windows even more daringly. By cladding the entire façade in glass, he creates, in effect, a curtain-wall, and in both the façade and the auditorium he exposes the cast-iron construction to make it a decorative as well as a functional element.

Victor Horta. Solvay house, Brussels. 1895–1900

Sullivan: Last Master of Architectural Ornament

Two years after the construction of the Maison du Peuple, Louis Sullivan (1856–1924) began to work on the Schlesinger-Meyer department store in Chicago. Although he failed to match the drama of Horta's curtain-wall, Sullivan did specify windows that were both larger and longer than those normally found in public buildings. They admitted light generously and, for that reason, came to be copied by designers of other public buildings in the Chicago area and so were called "Chicago windows." The enlargement of the windows to allow for the maximum amount of light required on the selling floors illustrates how Sullivan applied his popular dictum, "Form follows function," to his work.

The Schlesinger-Meyer store is starkly functional in its upper windows, but decorative in the wrought iron of its first two floors. Sullivan composed this plantlike ornament of scrolls, leaves and flowers and arranged it symmetri-

Victor Horta. Maison du Peuple, Brussels. 1897–1899

cally around doors and windows. Owing something to the flamboyant plant form decorating the columns of the late Gothic Southwell Cathedral in England, Sullivan's ornament achieves a three-dimensional, highly sculptural effect. In the Bayard building, Sullivan's only structure standing in New York, he included a terra-cotta frieze of pre-Raphaelite angels along the attic story.

Sullivan's greatest achievement was the creation of a suitable form for the tall office building, a new genre developed in response to the growing demands of commerce. Rather than disguise this new structure behind Greek, Roman or Romanesque decoration, Sullivan searched for a design that would express the fact that the building was an office for clerical workers. In the Guaranty Building he perfected the design he had been developing. Of the three layers of the building, the first consists of a reception floor and mezzanine, the second of ten floors of offices, the third of a decorated attic story and flat roof. Verticality, the overriding quality of the building, was emphasized by mullions that ran from mezzanine to roof without interruption. Spandrels were set back from mullions, so as not to spoil the effect of verticality. Ornament, though concentrated in the mullions, blossomed in the attic story to terminate the structure. Sullivan's finest free-standing skyscraper, it is a Whitmanesque hymn to American commerce.

Thirty-nine at the time he designed the Guaranty building, Sullivan experienced personal and professional hardship for the rest of his life. He received only twenty commissions over his last thirty years, among them five small banks in Ohio, Iowa, Wisconsin and Minnesota. The year he died he completed *The Autobiography of an Idea* and *A System of Architectural Ornament*.

Gaudi: First Master of Expressionist Architecture

Gaudí's biomorphic forms, undulating polychrome surfaces and brilliant structural innovations set his work apart from the mainstream of European architecture, yet he was perhaps the first developer of Art Nouveau motifs. For the Casa Vicens in Barcelona he designed an elaborate ironwork gate that may be the earliest example of Curvilinear. Executed in 1878, it predates Horta's Tassel House by four years and Mackmurdo's woodcut for *Wren's City Churches* by three years.

Family tradition in handcraftsmanship influenced Gaudí. Gaudí's father, a coppersmith, taught him to appreciate fine workmanship, and his architecture relied on the craft of Spanish ironworkers, masons and carpenters rather than on machine technology.

Gaudí was also influenced by the architecture in his native Catalonia. Bright color had been a tradition in Catalonian buildings since the ancient Greeks

Louis Sullivan. Schlesinger-Meyer Department store, Chicago. 1903–1904

Louis Sullivan. Schlesinger-Meyer Department store, ironwork, Chicago. 1903–1904

Louis Sullivan. Schlesinger-Meyer Department store, Chicago. Upper windows. 1903–1904

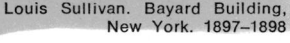

Louis Sullivan. Bayard Building, New York. 1897–1898

Auguste Perret. Garage, Paris. 1905

Peter Behrens. AEG Exposition Hall, Berlin. 1909

had colonized the region. The Casa Batlló, an early commission, was only a remodeling assignment. But by facing the walls and roof with iridescent tile, he bestowed on the entire building a unique personality. In the Parc Guell, Gaudí used color for a similar effect. This park, still popular with the citizens of Barcelona, was named after Gaudí's chief patron, the Spanish industrialist who commissioned him to design it. By embedding brightly colored tile in the undulating park benches, Gaudí created a tropical environment. The primordial quality of the Parc Guell, whether it disturbs or enchants, is without question different from the tamely Picturesque garden planned by Olmsted for Central Park (page 22).

Gaudí's penchant for tropical—even African—motifs is also evident in the finials for the Church of the Holy Family, his unfinished masterpiece. This church, on which Gaudí continued to work for the better part of his career, incorporates the three styles with which he was concerned. It is Gothic in its portals, Curvilinear in the upper portion of the façade and Rectilinear in its finials. Though Rectilinear in form, the unique finials probably derived from African sculpture.

The Church of the Holy Family also testifies to Gaudí's brilliance as an engineer. For added strength, Gaudí warped the surfaces of the tree-like interior columns and introduced hyperbolic paraboloid curves into the interior walls. The hyperbolic paraboloid curve is the one that any flexible object— for example, a piece of string—will take when suspended from two points. Because of its strength, this curve has been especially useful in making reinforced concrete shells strong despite their thinness. But Gaudí, though working in stone rather than concrete, used this curve brilliantly a half century before other architects had begun to use it for reinforced-concrete structures. Another engineering innovation in the Church of the Holy Family was tilted columns. Because the columns tilted to follow the direction of specific loads, they eliminated the need for buttresses. In the final scheme for the church Gaudí carried this solution a step further by specifying columns of different materials according to the differences in load they were intended to carry.

Reinforced Concrete: Harbinger of Modern Architecture

Auguste Perret (1874–1954), the French architect-engineer, showed both the domestic and the commercial possibilities of reinforced concrete. At 25 rue Franklin, Paris, Perret exposed the reinforced skeleton, cantilevered the upper stories over the street and made the structure float by dissolving the street floor into glass. These treatments were in advance of their time, and only the floral and pebble patterns of the ceramic-tile facing betray this building's Art Nouveau origin. In a garage on the rue Ponthieu, Perret also used reinforced concrete with an Art Nouveau motif, a rose window in the center of the façade. Not until 1920 would architects make unadorned reinforced concrete a trademark for the newly developing Functionalist mode of Modern architecture.

German and Austrian architects, by working in the Rectilinear rather than Curvilinear mode of Art Nouveau, placed themselves in the vanguard of the 20th-century stage of the Modern style. Peter Behrens exploited geometric, Functionalist forms in an exhibition hall for AEG. Less restrained, Josef Hoffmann covered the outside of the Stoclet House with marble plates framed in gilded bronze, but, except for the molding, he left exterior surfaces undecorated. Adolf Loos (1870–1933) removed every trace of ornament from the Steiner House. With roof flattened and windows of the rear façade placed asymmetrically, the Steiner House resembled a Mondrian painting. It is a last statement of Rectilinear Art Nouveau and a first statement of the Functionalist mode of the Modern style.

Antonio Gaudi. Casa Batlló, Barcelona. 1905–1907

Antonio Gaudi. Church of the Holy Family, Barcelona. 1885

Adolf Loos. Steiner House, Vienna. 1910

MODERN
DESIGN

The Functionalist
and Expressionist Traditions

R. Buckminster Fuller. Botanical Garden,
St. Louis, Mo. 1960

Antonio Sant'Elia. Project for a Futurist Town, Italy. 1913–1914

El Lissitzky and Mart Stam. Project for Cloud Props, U.S.S.R. 1924

Peter Cook. Project for a Plug-in Metropolis, England. 1967

Four important art movements helped shape Functionalist design early in the 20th century. Cubism, Futurism, Constructivism and de Stijl all appeared before World War I. Though separate movements with different leaders, they shared ideas and formal characteristics. In a revolution that took place between 1907 and 1914 Cubism reversed the Victorian emphasis, shifting it from content to form. Cézanne, the French precursor of Cubism, had urged artists to concentrate on cones, cubes, cylinders and spheres. Taking this as their cue, the Cubists then reduced natural objects to geometric shapes and reconstructed them as planes and solids.

Undecorated and geometric objects symbolized the new machine age. Like machinery, they tended to be smooth-surfaced and fabricated out of steel, rubber and other industrial materials. Traditionally, design sharing these characteristics has been called Cubist, Futurist or Constructivist, after the art movement that influenced it. The term Functionalist includes all 20th-century designs sharing these traits and, at the same time, alludes to the philosophy of Functionalism on which such design was built.

To prove that geometric shapes were "functional," that is, comfortable, inexpensive and easy to maintain and fabricate, designers quoted from a tangled mass of theory that did not always fit the facts. Loos's six-page essay, *Ornament and Crime* (1908), became the intellectual apology for the elimination of ornament from buildings and products.

The Futurist poet Marinetti held a conference in Russia in 1914. And the Russian Constructivists there discovered that they shared Futurist concern with function. Both groups dreamed of remaking the world in terms of the new technology. Cloud Props, envisioned by the Constructivist El Lissitzky, are Futurist in concept and super scale. Antonio Sant'Elia's similarly visionary project, Città Nuova, breathes much of the Constructivist spirit.

Lissitzky's "Cloud Prop" consisted of a simple geometric slab cantilevered from a vertical slab and illuminated with banded windows. The geometric form, the cantilever-construction principle and the window treatment soon became important elements in Functionalist architecture. Despite an ideological affinity with Futurism, the Constructivists found themselves closer to the Cubists in formal matters. Kasimir Malevich, influenced by Cubist abstraction, painted Eight Red Rectangles in 1915. This was the first painting with no source in nature and consisting of pure geometric forms.

The Constructivist International, founded in 1922, transmitted ideas to Holland where, four years earlier, designers had organized a movement called *de Stijl,* or the Style. Piet Mondrian and other de Stijl painters shared the high-color palette of the Constructivists and also a concern with abstract geometry. They avoided pastels in favor of primary shades of red, blue and yellow. And they proposed an architecture based on rectangular forms and asymmetrical balance, both of which emerge in the Schroeder House.

Archigram, a contemporary English group that proposes utopian solutions to contemporary city-planning problems, testifies to the continuing vitality of the Functionalist approach. In the project for Plug-in City they visualize an architectural future in which components from racks will be plugged into networks and grids. This adaptable mechanical environment includes separate cells for energy, information, entertainment, etc., that one adds to or rearranges at random. Instead of a city built by carpenters and masons, they see a city in which giant cranes will swing components into place. Plug-in University Node provides for information silos suspended at the top of structural pylons and teaching spaces clustered underneath. It accommodates itself to the rapidity with which the needs of a contemporary university change.

Expressionism, a secondary strain in 20th-century painting, was also a secondary strain in 20th-century design. The term designates the more romantic and spontaneous tendencies in modern art. In Germany the Expressionist movement converged on *Der Breucke,* the group formed in 1905 in Dresden that included the painters Emile Nolde and Ludwig Kirchner. A second German Expressionist group, *Der Blaue Reiter,* named after a work by the Russian painter Wassily Kandinsky, appeared in 1911 in Munich. The Expressionists emphasized content over form, feeling over reason. More concerned with human beings than with dynamos, they said in their Manifesto of 1905: "He who renders his inner convictions with spontaneity and sincerity is one of us."

Recent utopian projects confirm the continuing validity of Expressionist design. Paolo Soleri, an Italian architect living in America, has designed a "town on a table mountain" with forms that reflect the world of nature as tellingly as those of Archigram echo the world of technology. An American industrial designer, William Katavolos, proposes a chemical architecture in which furniture and buildings, "programmed" with special chemicals, would grow into forms specified by their designer. His sketches derive from the assumption that certain materials, such as plastic foams, can be programmed through chemical treatment. In the utopian technology of "grow-molding," structures will be neither sculpted out of whole material nor assembled out of separate parts but programmed to grow into predetermined forms.

The Japanese architects Kiyonori Kikutake, F. Maki and Noiaki Kureokawa (page 79) have proposed a new approach to city planning called Metabolic architecture. The Metabolists envision an architecture whose principles are analogous to those of biology, the science of life, because they believe "design and technology should be a denotation of human vitality." The Plant-type Community locates living space above ground and production or working space below ground. It borrows its forms from nature and its structural systems from biology.

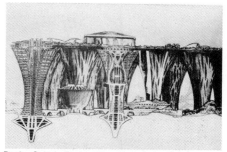

Paolo Soleri. Project for Biotechnic City, U.S.A. c. 1960

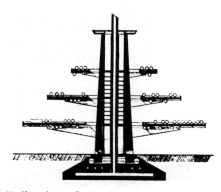

William Katavolos. Project for Chemical Architecture, U.S.A. c. 1960

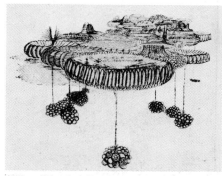

N. Kureokawa. Project for a plant-type community. Japan. 1960

Gerrit Rietveld. Schroeder house, Utrecht. 1924

Walter Gropius. Bauhaus, Dessau. 1925

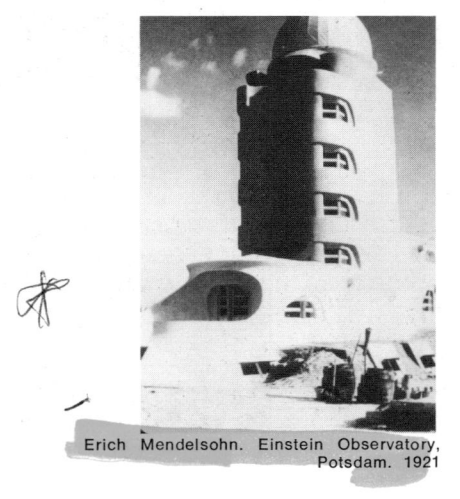

Erich Mendelsohn. Einstein Observatory, Potsdam. 1921

MODERN ARCHITECTURE

With all their diversity, 20th-century architects developed two major viewpoints. The Functionalist architects based their design on a philosophy of function and worked toward simple geometric forms and the elimination of ornament. The Expressionists, the second and less influential group, used masonry, carpentry and other handcraft processes rather than industrial ones and related their work to nature rather than the machine. The German architect Walter Gropius (1883–1970) aptly formulated the Functionalist mode in his design for the Bauhaus, the German design school he founded and directed. Located in Dessau and financed by a municipal appropriation, the Bauhaus building had three wings which housed 28 studio apartments, several baths, a dining hall and laundry, a school of design and workshops. A bridge, in which there were administrative rooms, club rooms and a private studio for Gropius, linked the school and workshop wings to the dormitory wing. In form each wing was a box, and the three of them were disposed asymmetrically, like the elements in a *de Stijl* composition. The flat roof, unframed windows and smooth, untextured stucco-surfaced walls reinforced the illusion that this was an exercise in solid geometry. In the workshop wing Gropius laid reinforced concrete floors and set back the mushroom posts that supported each floor in order to extend a glass façade for three stories without interruption. What Gropius had learned about glass walls when he was designing the Fagan Glassworks helped him in devising a glass screen of great dramatic scale for the Bauhaus. It foreshadowed the curtain-wall façades of the Lever House, the Seagram building and other post-World War II skyscrapers.

With a construction cost of only 20 cents per cubic foot, the Bauhaus was a remarkably practical design. Its gray-white concrete walls and hard, glittering glass façade related it to the world of technology. Its asymmetric floor plan, derived from the use to which space would be put rather than from an ideal of classic symmetry, related the Bauhaus to the new ideal of Functionalism. Paxton had foreshadowed the Functionalist mode in the Crystal Palace, an unselfconscious solution to a practical problem. Gropius distilled Paxton's approach into an identifiable architectural style and articulated it in the Bauhaus with unmatched coherence.

The Einstein Tower of Erich Mendelsohn (1887–1953) superbly realized the Expressionist ideal in architecture. An astronomical observatory that was to prove part of the theory of relativity, its sphere-topped tower appears to grow from the hill it rests on. Because the tower is balanced by two platforms of different heights, its silhouette, like that of a growing organism, is irregular. The biomorphic indentations around windows and doors, which might have been hollowed out by a sculptor's thumb, enhance the illusion of organic growth. Mendelsohn had planned the building in reinforced concrete, but because this material was too expensive in inflation-wracked post-war Germany, Mendelsohn substituted brick within the super-structure while stuccoing the outer walls to retain the effect of concrete.

Mendelsohn abandoned Expressionist architecture for the Functionalist manner soon after the tower was completed. The Schocken department stores, with their horizontal ribbon windows, represent Mendelsohn's later style. Columbus Haus, among the most attractive buildings in downtown pre-World War II Berlin, was a daring precursor to post-war curtain-wall skyscrapers. Mendelsohn immigrated to the United States in 1941. Here he designed seven synagogues that helped endow Jewish houses of worship with architectural significance for the first time since the Diaspora.

The 20th-Century House

Frank Lloyd Wright. Robie house, Chicago. 1909

Where the Victorian architect had designed a solid, ornamented building imitating an historic style, the architects Loos and Perret designed light, unornamented and ahistoric buildings in reinforced concrete. Using the same material, Corbusier raised the house off the ground. *Pilotis,* or free-standing columns, allowed the structure to hover airily in space. By means of the glass wall, Mies reunited the house with surrounding nature. By means of imaginative siting and natural materials, Wright made the house a part of nature. Thus was the Modern house, in large part, the work of three architectural giants: Le Corbusier, Ludwig Mies van der Rohe and Frank Lloyd Wright.

Le Corbusier. Villa Savoye, Poissy, France. 1927–1931

Frank Lloyd Wright (1869–1959) began practice in the 19th century and worked with Art Nouveau as well as Modern elements in the course of his long career. His earliest work, especially his furniture, was in the Rectilinear idiom of Art Nouveau. It also owed something to Louis Sullivan, his *"Lieber Meister,"* with whom Wright began to study in 1888. By 1910 Wright had developed the first of his Midwest Prairie houses, of which the Robie house was especially successful. Wright designed these low-slung houses with horizontal windows; on the inside conventional rooms were eschewed in favor of informal living areas. During the same decade Wright designed the glass-and-concrete Larkin office building in Buffalo. The Functionalist quality of this building, rather than the Expressionism of his houses, brought him to the attention of European architects.

With the exception of the huge, earthquake-proof Imperial Hotel in Tokyo, Wright produced less in the 1910–1920 decade than in the preceding ones. But in the 1920's he designed his own house, Taliesin, near Spring Green, Wisconsin. Appearing to grow out of its hillside site, faced with native lime-

Le Corbusier. Secretariat, Chandigarh (State of Punjab, Pakistan). 1950–1956

Le Corbusier. Chapel of Notre-Dame du Haut,
Ronchamp, France. 1950-1954

Ludwig Mies van der Rohe.
Farnsworth house, Plano, Ill. 1946-1950

Ludwig Mies van der Rohe. Seagram building,
New York. 1958

stone and glowing with warm earth colors, Taliesin fully realized Wright's "organic" approach to architecture. In 1936 Wright designed Falling Water (page 86), whose breathtaking cantilever attested to his mastery of reinforced concrete construction.

In the last 20 years of his career Wright built in virtually every region of the United States, using the desert of Arizona for his winter residence—Taliesin West—and the hills of Los Angeles for the Sturgis House. In the great glass dome of the Guggenheim Museum, Wright turned from assimilation of nature to imitation of its microstructure.

Charles-Edouard Jeanneret-Gris (1887–1965), known professionally as Le Corbusier, was as responsible as any individual for "the white architecture of the '20's." His innovations—the flat roof, the white, unornamented surfaces, the horizontal window, the free-standing column, the floating cube—permeated the ascetic "International Style" of the inter-war years. Le Corbusier, who had settled down to paint in Paris in 1917, devised a brand of Cubism that influenced his architecture, especially that of the Villa Savoye. A white Cubist painting in three dimensions, this "machine for living" captured the new spirit of the machine age.

Turning to the problems of urban planning in the 1930's, Le Corbusier suggested that multi-story villas set in open parks would prevent the city from sprawling without limit. Only after World War II could he put this concept into practice—in the Unites d'Habitation. This huge apartment complex was to be as influential as the Villa Savoye had been after World War I. His idea—to make a vertical garden city in which each family could have the pleasure of maximum privacy with the convenience of communal services—has been replicated in major cities around the world.

Le Corbusier's later work included the Ministry of Education for Rio de Janeiro, whose *brise-soleil,* or sun screen, was repeated in many South American buildings. In the buildings for the Punjab capital city, Chandigarh, Le Corbusier elaborated on ideas originated in the Unites d'Habitation. But in the fancifully sculptural Pilgrimage Church of Notre Dame du Haut, he gave way to Expressionism and an exciting use of color.

Ludwig Mies van der Rohe (1886–1969) brought Functionalist architecture to a classic perfection. Without formal training as an architect, Mies learned to appreciate craftsmanship from his father, a master mason. He apprenticed with Peter Behrens, from whom he learned to understand how the classic spirit might be re-expressed in terms of modern technology. Leaving Behrens in 1911, Mies set out to achieve his goal: "The creation of a modern architecture with a neo-classical severity of means, purity of form, perfection of proportions, elegance of detail and dignity of expression." But he waited nearly 15 years for his first important commission, the Berlin monument to Karl Liebknecht and Rosa Luxemburg. One of the few successful memorials designed in the century, it was destroyed by the Nazis.

By 1929 Mies had mastered the essential elements of his classic style, and the work of the ensuing years was continuing refinement of these concepts. His German Pavilion (page 86) for the International Exhibition in Barcelona, although open only one summer, became the single most important influence on 20th-century interior and furniture design. In 1930 Walter Gropius invited Mies to direct the Bauhaus. But seven years later, at the age of 50, Mies left Germany for the United States. The next year he joined the staff of the Illinois Institute of Technology and embarked on what was to be a highly successful American career. The glass-and-metal house for Dr. Edith Farnsworth, the buildings for Illinois Institute of Technology, and the monumental Seagram building are capstones for the Functionalist mode of 20th-century architecture.

Skidmore, Owings and Merrill—designers of Lever House, the Pepsi Cola and Union Carbide buildings and Chase Manhattan Bank in New York and of the Air Force Academy in Colorado Springs—and Philip Johnson, in the early stages of his architectural career, are among those most strongly influenced by Mies.

Robert Maillart. Tavanasa bridge, Switzerland. 1905

The Form-Givers

Engineers trained to exploit the properties of reinforced concrete, plastics and other synthetics have made more interesting advances in developing new forms than have architects.

The Swiss engineer Robert Maillart (1872–1940) was among the first to work with reinforced concrete, a material he treated with both economy and grace in more than 40 bridges, many over remote passes through the Swiss Alps. Maillart's most ingenious idea, which he introduced in 1905 at the Tavanasa Bridge over the Rhine, was to make the roadbed part of the vaulting system. By thus combining the functions of loading and bearing, Maillart achieved a remarkably pure form at low cost. Indeed, it was the economy of his bridges that won Maillart commissions. In appearance Swiss authorities found them too stark. Another Maillart innovation, for structures other than bridges, was the mushroom slab, in which he combined column and floor slab into a single element. His Cement Hall for the Swiss National Exhibition demonstrates the effectiveness of the parabolic curve in reinforced-concrete construction. Another principle developed by Maillart was the stiffened bar arch used first at the Val Tschiel bridge.

The French engineer Eugene Freyssinet (1879–1962) pioneered important technical improvements in reinforced concrete during the same years. Among

Robert Maillart. Schwandbach bridge, Switzerland. 1933

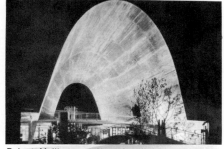

Robert Maillart and Hans Levsinger. Cement Hall, Swiss National Exhibition, Zurich. 1938–1939

Eugene Freyssinet. Hangars, Orley Field, Paris. 1916–1924

Eugene Freyssinet. Basilique Saint Piex, Lourdes. 1958

Pier Nervi. 181st Street Bus Station, New York. c. 1960

the first to understand the advantage of a parabolic curve, he used it to reduce tensile stress in aircraft hangars at Orly Field, Paris. By pleating the thin, reinforced-concrete vaults, Freyssinet gave them the necessary rigidity. In 1926 he began to experiment with the tensile stressing of the metal reinforcements embedded in concrete. This led to his patenting of prestressed reinforced concrete in 1928. The greater freedom and slenderness of form provided by prestressing are used to advantage in La Route National 67 and in the underground Basilica of Pius X at Lourdes. His work has especially influenced Eduardo Torroja.

Only a year after Freyssinet took out his patent for prestressed concrete, the Spanish structural engineer Eduardo Torroja (1889–1961) used it for his Tempul bridge. That he had mastered this innovation was demonstrated in the shell roof of the Fronton Recoletos, the X-shaped pipeline supports of the Aldoz aqueduct, the cantilevered roof of the Zarzuela race track near Madrid and the Martin Gil bridge over the Esla. The latter's 623-foot span broke the world's record for a single-arch bridge.

The Italian engineer Pier Luigi Nervi (1891–   ) ranks with Freyssinet and Maillart in his ability to create—from mathematical calculations and from the nature of his materials—virtually perfect geometric forms. Nervi has developed a system of on-site prefabrication and hydraulic prestressing for reinforced concrete, his favorite material. At the Turin Exhibition building and New York Port Authority bus terminal, he developed techniques for lightening roofs and for strengthening them through corrugation. Perhaps the finest exhibition hall since the Crystal Palace, the Turin structure has been ranked second only to Corbusier's Unites d'Habitation as the most important building in post-war Europe. Other major Nervi buildings are the Communal Stadium at Florence (consisting of nothing but exposed structural elements) and the aircraft hangar at Orvieto.

The Spanish-born engineer Felix Candela (1910–   ), influenced by the earlier pioneers in reinforced concrete, has become a leading designer of shell structures. For the University City in Mexico, to which Candela migrated after fighting with the Republicans in the Spanish Civil War, he designed the Cosmic Ray building. The roof of this building is a series of hyperbolic paraboloids, and the strength of the shape enabled him to reduce roof thickness to $5/8$ of an inch. The parabolic vault, unlike other types, can be poured into shuttering made from straight boards with considerable savings in materials costs. Among Candela's other important commissions have been the Church of the Miraculous Virgin and the Stock Exchange in Mexico City.

Richard Buckminster Fuller (1895–   ), Harvard drop-out and coiner of a colorful if eccentric design vocabulary, towers as the patriarch of American design after a lifetime of fighting for unconventional solutions to unconventional problems. Largely self-taught, Fuller operates more like a mathematician than like an engineer or architect. His most remarkable structure, the geodesic dome, is derived from mathematical calculations. It provides the greatest enclosed space in relation to the surface area of the enclosed form. The dome consists of a rigid frame made by joining many separate rods into small interconnected triangles. The frame may be covered with metal, plastic, cardboard or other materials. The U. S. government erected geodesic domes for exhibition buildings at the Brussels World's Fair and at Expo '67 in Montreal. Fuller's machine for living, the Dymaxion (dynamic plus maximum efficiency) House, and machine for transportation, the three-wheeled Dymaxion car, also achieve maximum use from minimum material and space.

The German designer Frei Otto continues to pioneer some of the most interesting structural experiments, especially with suspended roofs, tents (such as the one he erected for the German Pavilion at Expo '67) and inflated plastic structures.

Felix Candela. Cosmic Ray Laboratory, University of Mexico, Mexico. c. 1960.

R. Buckminster Fuller. Geodesic dome, U.S.A. 1954

Frei Otto. German Pavilion, Expo '67, Montreal. 1967

Ludwig Mies van der Rohe, German Pavilion,
Barcelona Exposition. 1929

Ludwig Mies van der Rohe. Tugendhat house,
Brno, Czechoslovakia. 1930

Frank Lloyd Wright. Falling Water,
Bear Run, Pa. 1936

20th-CENTURY INTERIOR DESIGN

Mies van der Rohe, chief architect of the 20th-century interior, was first to conceive the Functionalist room. He demonstrated his idea in the German Pavilion for the Barcelona Exposition of 1929 and, less than a year later, assembled similar interiors for the Tugendhat house, a private residence. In both cases, Mies insisted that the building interior had to be congruent with the exterior. Victorians had been oriented toward the past, and their interiors, with neo-Gothic or neo-Egyptian trim, proved it. Literally up-to-date, the 20th-century family wanted no reminder of the past in its furnishings. Contrasting the Tugendhat living room with the garden by means of a glass wall, Mies dramatized the differences between his rationally planned, machinelike room and the natural world of the garden. The Tugendhat house also demonstrated the new importance of industrial materials in the home. To make steel and glass as acceptable in the domestic setting as in a factory, Mies juxtaposed them with travertine and other luxury materials. He enhanced a white linoleum floor with a living-room wall of gold-trimmed white onyx and a dining-room wall of striped black-and-pale-brown Macassar ebony. The effect was coldly handsome.

As the Tugendhat house launched Functionalist interior design, so Frank Lloyd Wright's houses established Expressionist or, to use his word, organic, interior design. For private houses Wright used wood, stone and other natural materials instead of the steel and glass favored by Mies. Where Mies's interior was ascetically monochromatic, Wright's glowed with warm, earth colors. The simplicity and comfort of Falling Water are the antithesis of the sumptuous austerity of the Tugendhat house. The walls at Falling Water are made of stained lumber or stone from the surrounding hills. Victorian designers had imitated nature, but Wright assimilated it at Falling Water.

Whether Functionalist or Expressionist, Modern interiors shared more with one another than with Victorian interiors. The Victorian home had been an enclosed fortress; the Modern house was open to nature. The Victorian interior had been dark and cluttered; the Modern interior was light and sparsely furnished. Victorian furniture had been ponderous; Modern furniture was light. Interest centered on sculptural form, rather than carved surfaces. Light beamed from invisible sources, and lighting fixtures became, like the chair, highly sculptural. The Victorian home boasted dining-room, pantry, music-room and library; the Modern home dissolved these rooms into loosely defined areas for play, study and eating. Only bathroom and kitchen retained their identity as separate rooms. The new designers replaced patterned wallpaper with smooth white walls or with wood, brick or stone in order to maximize the effect of texture, rather than pattern.

To achieve the new look in interiors, designers needed components more simple than any previously manufactured. By the 1940's housewares imported from Denmark, Finland and Italy were sold in the United States by Design Research, Georg Jensen and Bonnier's. An American firm, Knoll Associates, founded by Hans and Florence Knoll, began to manufacture furniture by Mies, Breuer, Le Corbusier, Saarinen and Bertoia in 1946. By mid-1960, Knoll Associates had opened showrooms in a dozen American cities and a number of foreign countries. Another key American manufacturer was Herman Miller, who produced furniture by George Nelson and Charles Eames.

Frank Lloyd Wright. Wooden chair, U.S.A. 1904

Misconceptions about Modern Chairs

Misconception befogs the history of the Modern chair. The public equates the Modern chair with comfort. But, with important exceptions, the Modern chair is not comfortable. The strict angles of the Rietveld chair make no concession to human anatomy. The Barcelona chair is uncomfortably large, except for large-framed adults, such as Mies himself. The low tilt of the Hardoy chair militates against graceful sitting or rising. Indeed, the assumption that a chair should be comfortable is peculiar to recent times. Beautiful as they were, Egyptian, Greek and Roman chairs were not comfortable. Essentially thrones, these chairs enhanced the sitter's dignity rather than easing his back.

Gerrit Rietveld. Wooden chair, Holland. 1917

In addition to the delusion about comfort, the public has a false notion that the Modern chair is functional, and defines function as ease of maintenance, ease of production and low cost. But the owner of a Modern chair may spend as much time caring for it as for a Chippendale. He polishes the tubular steel classics of the 1920's to prevent tarnishing. He guards the newer plastic chairs from bending, breaking and scarring. What about ease of production? The Barcelona chair, epitome of Functionalist design, still requires hand labor, although its manufacturer has had more than a generation in which to work out a factory technique. Hand labor accounts in part for the price of the Barcelona chair; at $900 retail, it costs more than any chair in serial production. Why does the public pay so much for a chair that is not comfortable? The owner's expenditure attests to his good taste. Also the Barcelona chair, as a ritual object, effectively enhances the authority of its owner.

Cubist Chairs

The story of the Modern chair is the story of the designer's successful adoption of one new material after another—first tubular steel, then plywood, then

Marcel Breuer. Wooden chair, Germany. 1922

Alvar Aalto. Molded plywood chair,
Finland. 1934

Marcel Breuer. Tubular steel chair,
Germany. 1924

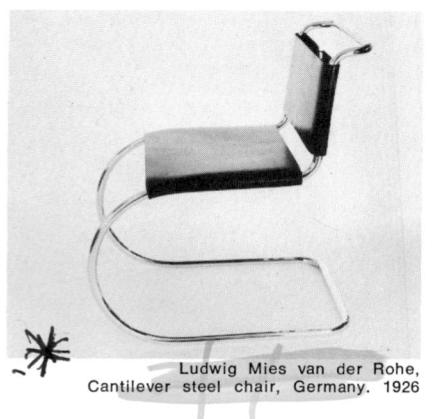

Ludwig Mies van der Rohe,
Cantilever steel chair, Germany. 1926

Ludwig Mies van der Rohe.
Barcelona chair, 1929

Le Corbusier. Revolving tubular steel chair,
France. 1927

Antonio Bonet and Juan Korchan.
Hardoy chair, Argentina. 1938

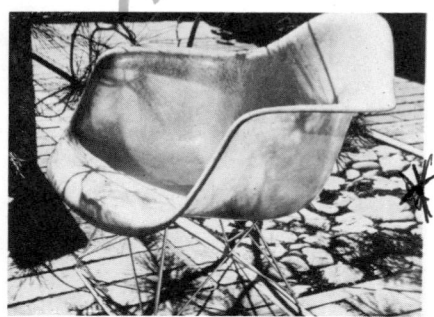

Charles Eames. Molded fiberglass chair,
U.S.A. 1951

Eero Saarinen. "Womb" chair,
U.S.A. 1948

Eero Saarinen. Molded fiberglass chair,
U.S.A. 1957

Ludwig Mies van der Rohe.
Cantilever steel chair, Germany. 1927

Marcel Breuer. Cantilever steel chair,
Germany. 1928

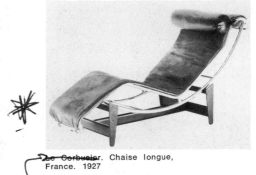

Le Corbusier. Chaise longue,
France. 1927

CHARLOTTE PERRIAND

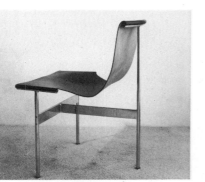

William Katavolos, Douglas Kelley and
Ross Littell. T-frame tubular steel chair,
U.S.A. 1952

Harry Bertoia. Wire frame chair,
U.S.A. 1952

Charles Eames. Molded plywood .chair,
U.S.A. 1946

Laverne staff design. Plexiglass chair,
U.S.A. 1958

Gunnar Anderson. Urethane foam chair,
Denmark. 1964

Verner Panton. Inflatable plastic chair,
Denmark. 1964.

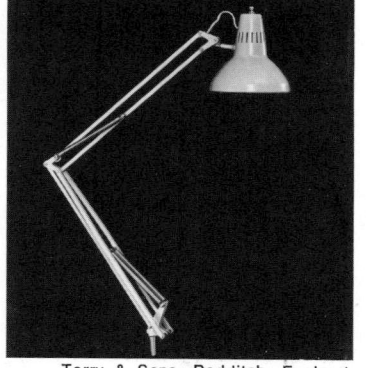

Terry & Sons, Redditch, England,
and Jac Jacobsen, Oslo.
Drafting lamp, Luxo Lamp Corp.,
Port Chester, N. Y. 1937

Peter Pfisterer. Desk Lamp, Germany, 1946

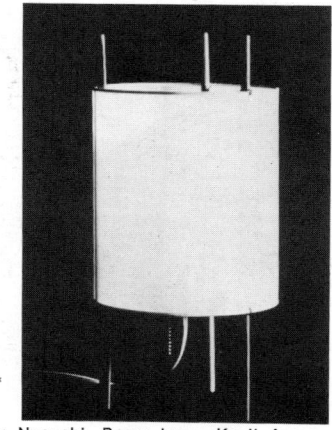

Isamu Noguchi. Paper lamp, Knoll Assoc.,
U.S.A. 1947

polyester resin and, in the last decade, polyurethane foam. Wright designed the first important 20th-century chairs. Though he selected wood, the most conventional of materials, he came up with forms that were new. In their awkward boxiness Wright's chairs resembled Cubist sculptures. Though less graceful, they also resembled Mackintosh's discreetly decorated chairs.

Wright's furniture began to be appreciated in Europe soon after 1910. At the request of a client for chairs similar to Wright's, the Dutch architect Gerrit Thomas Rietveld (1888–   ) designed a similar de Stijl chair. Though Rietveld's chair, like Wright's, is based on geometric forms, the effect is different. This is because Rietveld bases his design on the de Stijl principle of asymmetrical balance and follows the red, blue and black de Stijl color scheme. Rietveld imbued the chair with an appearance of weightlessness by separating supporting from supported parts. The Museum of Modern Art has called it "an uncommonly ugly" chair, but it teaches a splendid lesson in de Stijl principles.

De Stijl filtered into the Bauhaus, where the Hungarian-born designer Marcel Breuer (1902–   ) worked first as a student and then as director of the furniture workshop. Breuer continued in the direction mapped out by Wright and Rietveld, coming up with yet another version of the wooden chair based on geometric forms.

Breuer's greatest importance lies in his pioneering investigation of tubular steel. Tubular steel was the first 20th-century industrial material to be used in a chair, and Breuer was the first to use it. His double contribution is that, by using the metals associated with machines as well as the geometric forms associated with them, he gave a machine-like quality to the chair. Breuer came up with the idea of tubular-steel furniture after noticing the chromium-plated tubular-steel handlebars of his bicycle. Breuer urged Adler, a German bicycle maker, to manufacture tubular-steel-framed chairs and tables. But the company feared that chromium-plated furniture would repel the public, and Breuer, on his own, designed a prototype with fabric seat and back and folding armrests. In a second, still popular version, Breuer substituted a double-S-shaped support for the conventional four legs. This eliminated many joints and gave the chair comfortable resiliency. During the '20's decade, Breuer, Mies and Corbusier each designed chairs which are still produced and often cited as classic examples of Functionalist furniture.

The Resilient Cantilever

In late 1927 the Dutch architect Mart Stam introduced the cantilever principle in a tubular steel chair exhibited at the Werkbund Exhibition in Stuttgart. This principle allowed the designer, by altering the conventional center of balance, to eliminate the chair's rear legs. At the same exhibition Mies also showed a cantilever steel chair. Because of its resiliency, Mies's chair was considered superior to the Stam chair which had a stiff frame linked together by standard pipe joints. Breuer's cantilever chair followed the next year. Le Corbusier, also in 1927, designed a tubular-steel, adjustable chaise longue. Like the Unites d'Habitation, it hovered above the ground on sculptured stilts. Tubular steel was further explored in the next generation when William Katavolos, Ross Littell and Douglas Kelley designed a T-form chair. The most popular tubular metal chair, the Hardoy, consisted of only a continuous metal frame and a pouch of leather or fabric. Originally adapted from an Italian officer's chair, it has been copied by dozens of furniture manufacturers, who sometimes sell it for less than $10. A more recent tubular metal chair, designed by the sculptor Harry Bertoia, consists of cloth cushions and a frame encased in rubber like a dish drain. An indeterminate number of components go into the frame.

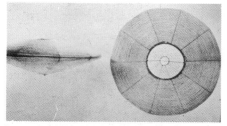

Isamu Noguchi. Akari ceiling lamps, U.S.A. c. 1955

The Molded Plywood Chair

In the decade after the first experiments with tubular steel, molded plywood aroused the interest of furniture designers. The Finnish architect Alvar Aalto (1898–   ), who had designed a tubular-steel sofa-bed in 1930 and wooden furniture for the Paimio Sanatorium in 1932, developed a successful design and production technique for plywood early in the 1930's. Wood-bending and wood-laminating had been practiced by the 19th-century designers Michael Thonet and John Belter, and lightweight plywood seats supported by metal springs had been used for decades in trolley cars. Achieving a similar, though more elegant, effect with Finnish birch, Aalto worked out a technique for laminating and molding wood in thin layers of veneer and of stamping out chair parts much as cookies are stamped from a sheet of dough.

George Nelson. Bubble lamps, Howard Miller Clock Co., Zeeland, Mich. 1952

Charles Eames (1907–   ), in his painstaking development of a single chair design over a six-year period, illustrates the degree to which successful furniture design depends on successful fabricating techniques. In collaboration with the architect Eero Saarinen, Eames won the 1940 Museum of Modern Art furniture-design contest. The winning chair was unusual not so much because it was made of plywood as because it curved in two planes rather than one. The aircraft industry had developed a technique for the compound curving of plywood, and Eames believed it would prove both inexpensive and simple for the production of plywood chairs. It was neither. For the next six years Eames studied the problem of how to bring down the cost of the metal

Irving Harper. Modular lamp, U.S.A. c. 1967

mold from which each plywood shell was to be stamped. But the American furniture industry of the 1940's had neither the stamping, the bonding nor the binding techniques to manufacture the chair. In 1945 Eames scrapped the metal-mold production technique as well as the one-piece shell design. As an alternative, he designed a chair with separately molded seat and back. For this design he invented machines for pressing plywood, borrowed the idea of rubber shock mounts from the auto industry and the idea of electronic welding from the aircraft industry. Redesigned, the chair was again exhibited at the Museum of Modern Art in 1946. The Herman Miller Company, which markets the chair at $32 wholesale, has sold more than 1,000,000 since then.

The Plastic Chair

What tubular steel had been to the 1930's and plywood to the 1940's, reinforced fiberglass was to the 1950's. And Eames, with a new resin called Zenaloy, was at last able to fabricate the one-piece plywood shell chair originally designed for the museum competition.

Saarinen, Eames's collaborator on the competition chair, also designed a reinforced fiberglass chair. The tulip-shaped shell is reminiscent of the competition chair, but the flowerlike stem avoids the distracting wire-cage base of Eames's plastic chair. The Saarinen chair rebuts the cold precision line of the tubular steel chairs of the 1930's with a highly sculptural biomorphic form, a form quite differently expressed in Anderson's urethane-foam chair (page 89).

The Rational Kitchen

Although the introduction of gas and electric power provided designers the chance to simplify the work of the housewife, the first concerted effort to improve kitchen-equipment design did not come until the Depression. Then equipment manufacturers began to redesign their lines in order to boost sales. In 1932 General Electric and Westinghouse opened cooking institutes to investigate how to improve kitchen design. As a result of suggestions from cooks, engineers and architects, the institutes came up with a new room arrangement in which stove, sink, refrigerator and cabinets were lined up against one wall. The next important advance in kitchen design came in 1946 when Thermador announced a stove designed, not as a separate unit, but as part of the architecture of the kitchen. Thermador's built-in-oven went directly into the wall, while the range unit, with burners set into a sheet of

Staff design. Built-in oven. Thermador, Los Angeles. 1946.

George Nelson. Storage wall, Herman Miller Furniture Co., Zeeland, Mich. 1949

Robert Blee and Arthur BecVar. Kitchen center, General Electric Co., Louisville, Ky. 1956

stainless steel, plugged into the countertop. In 1955 General Electric designers put the finishing touch on the trend toward built-in units with a kitchen in which stove, refrigerator and sink were all part of the architecture.

The Functional Bathroom

Designers began to modernize the bathroom in the 1930's, but even the most serious of these early designs, such as one made by Le Corbusier, tended more toward decoration than functionalism. Le Corbusier, with his cousin, Pierre Jenneret, and Charlotte Perrand, designed a "sanitary cabin" for E-tablissement Delafond. They scaled each fixture according to the Modular, a series of harmonic measurements based on human proportions. To show that an efficient bathroom could be composed of a few parts, Corbusier fitted into a 49-inch space a wash basin and a toilet. A long, swiveling nozzle above the wash basin emptied into a wood-slat floor, beneath which an enamelled cast-iron sub-floor acted as a drain. Corbusier's "machine for bathing and elimination" was more Functionalist than functional. Evidence for this is the discrepancy between the scale and placement of Corbusier's fixtures and the scale and placement of those published in Alexander Kira's *Criteria for Bathroom Design* (1967). This volume scientifically scales sink, toilet and tub for the first time and places them in terms of comfort, safety and maintenance. It grew from a five-year Cornell University study.

Le Corbusier. Bathroom, Etablissement Delafond, France. 1936

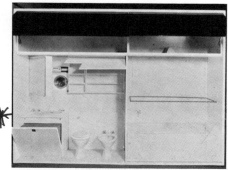

Richard Sapper, Luigi Caramella, Giamaria Beretta. Prefabricated bath unit in enameled sheet steel, Sentes, Turin, Italy. 1969

The greatest obstacle in the way of improved contemporary bathrooms is production rather than design. For decades it has been technically possible to extrude or mold an entire bathroom, including sink, toilet and other fixtures, into one or two pieces of plastic shell. However, plumbing and construction trades unions feared that such pre-assembled bathrooms would curtail the need for their services. And American manufacturers, especially, have been slow to buck the unions by producing single-shell or multi-shell bathroom units. The Crane, the Italian Santes, and others coming on the market in the 1970's, though theoretically less expensive because fabricated into fewer pieces, still cost more than a conventionally outfitted bathroom.

Staff design. Unette packaged bathroom, four piece fiberglass shell. Crane Canada Ltd., Canada. 1967.

INDUSTRIAL DESIGN

In post-1917 Russia, where the notion of designing products for an unchained proletariat was warmly received, young Constructivists forged the geometric forms that were to dominate product design for twenty years. Some Constructivists, all of whom were Communists, followed Kasimir Malevich (1878–1935), who said that art by its nature was nonfunctional and that industrial design was a second-rate activity. A second group followed Vladimir Tatlin (1885–1953) and Alexander Rodchenko (1891–1956), who held the artist to be a technician in the use of the machines and materials of modern industry. In Tatlin's view, work was to become art. Technique was to replace style. This conception won out; the name Constructivism stuck; and the group's art became known as "production art." In spite of their theoretical rejection of style, the Constructivists developed a powerful look characterized by abstraction, asymmetry, geometricity and horizontality.

The discrepancy between the utilitarianism of Constructivist theory and the impracticality of proposed designs opened the group's work to ridicule. Tatlin's Monument to the Third International was typical of their unfeasible but grand designs. Within a steel spiral, a glass cylinder was to serve as a convention hall, a glass cone as executive office and a cube as information center. Each unit rotated once a year, once a month and once a day, respectively. On overcast nights the information center was meant to project mottoes directly onto the clouds. Stunningly impractical, Tatlin's unrealized project remains a monument to the imagination and daring of the Constructivists.

While Tatlin explored the possibilities of constructing with metal, the Hungarian Laszlo Moholy-Nagy (1895–1946) began construction with light. *Lichtrequisit,* 1922–1930, a light sculpture, was powered by a motor in its base that also illuminated more than one hundred colored bulbs. These flashed at and through the sculpture in a two-minute cycle, throwing moving patterns of light on nearby surfaces. *Lichtrequisit* was the first light sculpture as well as the first kinetic sculpture.

The Bauhaus

While the work of most Constructivists had been largely experimental, designers at the Bauhaus made it practical. The same may be said of the efforts of the Dutch de Stijl group, many of whose members visited or lectured at the Bauhaus. This German school taught, for the first time, how to fashion light fixtures, furniture, housewares and other products into Constructivist and de Stijl forms. The development of a vocabulary of forms, based on Construc-

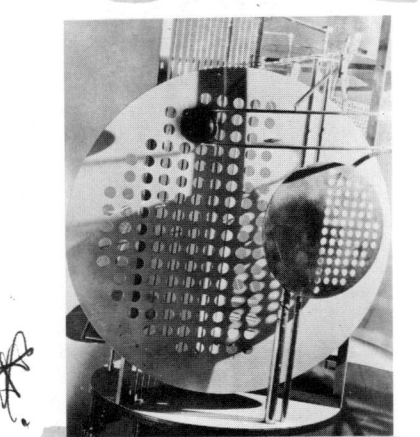

Vladimir Tatlin.
Monument to the Third International.
Russia. 1919–1920

Laszlo Moholy-Nagy. Mobile light sculpture, Germany. 1922–1930

tivist and de Stijl experiments, was perhaps the most significant achievement of the Bauhaus. These forms have influenced design throughout the Western world for two generations. And the remarkable Bauhaus faculty influenced American as well as German design instruction. After the school closed in 1933, Walter Gropius and Marcel Breuer taught at Harvard, Mies and Moholy-Nagy at Illinois Institute of Technology and Josef Albers at Yale.

In addition to the development of new forms, the Bauhaus developed a special method for training artists and craftsmen for machine production. The Bauhaus provided parallel courses of instruction in materials and in theories of form. In the early years the student was taught by two masters, one an artist and the other a craftsman. Instruction began with a six-month course in which the student worked with stone, wood, metal, clay, glass, pigments and textiles.

Gropius, the school's first director, insisted that students explore the nature and potential of materials by learning the crafts associated with each. Only after truly understanding the material was the student considered ready to design for machine production. In the course devoted to form, students learned how to draw. They also studied geometry, building construction, composition and color theory. One of the first advocates of teamwork in architecture and industrial design, Gropius anticipated that only this approach would be adequate to the technological complexities of machine production.

In spite (or because) of the school's success, the conservative Weimar city government pressured Gropius to close it, and in 1925 he moved it to Dessau, center of the German chemical industry and home of the Junkers airplane factory. Directed in the final days by Mies, the Bauhaus closed in 1933. The Nazis later used the Gropius-designed building as a school for political training. Retaining part of the old curriculum, the *Hochschule fur Gestaltung,* or New Bauhaus, opened at Ulm in 1955, initially under the direction of the Swiss designer Max Bill (1908–   ).

In 1951 Dr. Fritz Eichler vigorously revived the Bauhaus tradition of rationally analyzing structure into component geometric forms at the Braun Company. Under his direction, radios, phonographs, hair dryers and the firm's other electric appliances were transformed into similarly designed boxes. Braun designers arranged handles, buttons and dials in parallel lines and maintained right angles at all corners. They achieved economy by using a single medium for several jobs. Legs served as handles. Grilles provided surface decoration. Wilhelm Wagenfeld and Max Bill are other contemporary Europeans who design in the Functionalist mode established at the Bauhaus.

Wilhelm Wagenfeld and J. Jucker. Table lamp, Bauhaus, Germany. 1923–1924

Gerrit Rietveld. Table Lamp, Holland. 1924

Detail of catalog for factories manufacturing Bauhaus-designed lighting, Germany. c. 1924

Wilhelm Wagenfeld. Flatware,
Germany. 1952

Marianne Brandt. Teapot, Bauhaus,
Germany. 1924

Staff design. Hair dryer, Braun Co.,
Germany. c. 1965

Futurism and Italian Design

Italian industrial designers picked up esthetic theory as well as lessons in form from Futurist painters and sculptors. Motion fascinated the Futurist artists, and this, in turn, influenced the form that industrially designed objects would take. Balla (page 53) and other Futurist painters described motion in much the way Marey and Muybridge (page 53) had recorded it in stop-motion photos. Futurist sculpture—for example, Umberto Boccioni's *Unique Forms of Continuity in Space*—re-created the experience of motion in a still sculpture. This sense of motion seeped into architecture and consumer products, where corners, instead of meeting at right angles, tapered into a stream line. The Olivetti Lettera (page 98), the Necchi Mirella, the Vespa, the CisItalia resemble Futurist sculpture in their fluid forms. This sculptural elegance opposes the geometric forms of German design. Moreover, the Italian designer tends to sheathe his products in an envelope while the German articulates each part separately. In terms of shape and line, Futurism advanced the Expressionist mode of industrial design.

Gio Ponti (1891–   ), designer of the Pirelli and Montecantini office buildings in Milan and of the ministry buildings in Pakistan's Islamabad, introduced Italy to Modern industrial design when, in 1923, he exhibited ceramics at the first Triennale, Italy's international exhibition of industrial design and architecture. Since then Ponti has designed cutlery for Krupp and for Christofle as well as architectural components and furniture. Ponti founded *Domus* in 1928 to promote modern interior design. He also founded the short-lived *Stile Industria* to promote Italian industrial design.

In 1936 Adriane Olivetti retained Marcello Nizzoli, designer of an influential exhibit at the 1934 Italian Aeronautical Exposition, to direct design at Olivetti. Nizzoli's design for the Olivetti Lettera 22 established the firm's reputation for excellence in design. In later typewriters and in the Summa Prima 20 adding machine Nizzoli switched to geometric forms. When Olivetti entered the computer field in 1956, it retained Ettore Sottsass, Jr., to design Elea, a rational, architecturally unified electronic data-processing system. Complementing Olivetti's industrial design program is an architectural program led by Luigi Figini and Gino Fellini and a graphic design program led by Giovanni Pinteri. Other important Italian industrial designers are the Castiglioni Brothers, Marco Zanuso, G. Columbini, Alberto Rosselli, former editor of *Stile Industria,* and Pinin Farina, the automobile designer.

The Futurist theory of esthetics also influenced the Functionalist mode of industrial design. Socrates had said that a dung basket can be beautiful and a golden shield ugly according to whether each has been made well or badly for its special purpose. From this comment the Futurists derived the belief that beauty results automatically from perfect mechanical efficiency. The poet F. T. Marinetti proclaimed in the Futurist Manifesto (1909) that "a racing motor car, its frame adorned with great pipes . . . is more beautiful than the Victory of Samothrace." A decade later Corbusier compared the automobile to the Parthenon and envisioned the house as a machine for living. Antonio Sant'Elia's Cittá Nuova, or new city, forecasts a Futurist metropolis whose concrete-glass-and-steel skyscrapers would fit into a present-day city. Sant'-Elia sought to abolish academic architecture in Italian cities. A dynamo, rather than a human heart, powered the new city; technology, rather than nature, provided the new environment. Sant 'Elia's sketches included elevators placed on the outside of buildings and multi-level streets joined to one another by escalators. An early proponent of planned obsolescence, Sant'-Elia also believed in a "throw-away" esthetic. "Houses will not last as long as we. Every generation should build its own city," he said.

Umberto Boccioni.
Unique Forms of Continuity in Space,
Italy. 1919

Marketing Men in a Marketing Town

A year before the Armory Show began to influence American painting, John Cotton Dana's 1912 exhibition of German Applied Art at the Newark Museum began to influence American industrial design. In 1912 the term industrial design had not been coined. By 1920 an American named Joseph Sinel had stamped it on his letterhead. In 1912 no American school offered instruction in industrial design. By 1960, 20 American colleges and universities offered degree programs in the discipline. Some were art schools, including Art Center School in Los Angeles, the Chicago Art Institute, Cranbrook Academy of Art in Michigan and Rhode Island School of Design. Some like Georgia Tech and Carnegie Tech were engineering institutes. And some were universities, including Syracuse, California and Michigan. In 1912 only Germany had a professional industrial-design society. In 1938 Walter Dorwin Teague, Raymond Loewy and Henry Dreyfuss formed the Industrial Designer's Institute, since merged with the American Society of Industrial Design.

Marco Zanuso. Sewing machine, Borletti, Milan. 1956

American industrial design got its start during the Depression of the 1930's when desperate manufacturers asked Norman Bel Geddes, Raymond Loewy, Walter Dorwin Teague and Henry Dreyfuss to restyle their products in order to boost sales. As marketing men in a marketing nation, Bel Geddes and Loewy lent dash to the new calling. Teague made it respectable. In 1922 Teague sued the United States government for an income-tax rebate on the grounds that he was a professional rather than a businessman. Teague won the suit, the first step in establishing professional status for industrial designers. Nevertheless, industrial designers do not agree as to what they pro-

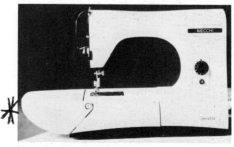
Marcello Nizzoli. Sewing machine, Necchi, Italy. 1956

Marcello Nizzoli. Olivetti Lettera 22 portable typewriter, Italy. 1950

Staff design. IBM typewriter, U.S.A. 1947

George Rehklau. Portable tape recorder, Ampex Corp., Redwood City, Calif. 1954

fess nor have they followed other professions in establishing licensing requirements. Among the other pioneer industrial designers are Charles Eames, Eliot Noyes, Russel Wright, Eva Zeisel, Harley Earl, Jon Hauser and Jay Doblin.

The Dematerialization of the Product

The Age of the Product ended after World War II with the industrial designer's search to dispose, conceal, miniaturize and otherwise dematerialize consumer products. Kimberly Clark's Kleenex made disposability a desirable aim in the 1930's. Since then manufacturers have built disposability into plates, dresses, tents, chairs, bandages, hypodermic syringes and fountain pens, and they have repackaged milk and other beverages in more easily disposed of cartons. In 1946 radio, phonograph and other living-room appliances disappeared into the storage wall (page 92). The transistor eliminated the bulky vacuum tube and reduced the radio to the size of a cigar case and the TV set to the size of an overnight bag.

Dematerialization occurs when a single product is replaced by a system, for example, when a wall of heated air replaces a department-store door, when a built-in, suction-based cleaning system replaces a vacuum cleaner or when a luminescent ceiling replaces a lamp. Thus, industrial design has become a matter of packaging. The best contemporary American product design (*vide* the Ramac computer or the Edison Voicewriter) consists of encasing complex electronic parts in boxes that are as unobtrusive and easy to operate as possible.

The Industrialization of Architecture

In this century, architecture has become increasingly a matter of industrial design. At the Bauhaus, as early as 1921, Gropius explored means of mass-producing houses by standardizing the size of component parts. In 1946 Konrad Wachsman utilized the principle of serial production in designing an aircraft hangar whose space frame was built up from modular steel members. Habitat, designed for Expo '67, demonstrated how serial production could be adapted to reinforced concrete, as Russian architects had done successfully since the end of World War II. With the availability of mail-order, factory-made geodesic domes, the building *became* a product. While the architect remained prisoner of a single patron, the industrial designer, like the filmmaker and fashion photographer, permeated mass society with his work. Nevertheless, the most stylistically significant products were designed by architects, such as Gio Ponti, George Nelson and Charles Eames.

With these developments, American industrial designers shifted in the 1960's from product design to product planning, space planning, systems analysis and other activities related to services rather than goods. The Walter Dorwin Teague office, for example, has simplified manufacturing procedure for the U. S. Navy's aircraft electronic wiring system with a technique called value analysis.

Environmental Design

As the 1970's unfold, industrial designers seek to reshape the nature of their work toward socially meaningful services. In response to the environmental crisis choking the country, industrial designers have begun to join forces with architects, engineers and environmental scientists in what amounts to the forging of a new field: environmental design.

Decay in inner cities and a population that will reach 300 million by the year 2000, together with tremendous technical capability, have led to design projects having an unprecedentedly vast scale—new urban transportation systems, new medical centers, even entire new towns. Because of their vast scale, these projects are complex and require for successful execution not the talent of a single genius but the concerted effort of a team of design professionals. Increasingly, the industrial designer, like the architect and engineer, is taking his place on an environmental design team, one that may include sociologists and psychologists as well as physical scientists.

What distinguishes the environmental designer from the older design professionals is not so much a set of new skills as an amalgam of attitudes. The environmental designer knows that technological improvement may bring unforeseen harm. He views the environment not as a collection of parts but as a total fabric susceptible to design at a regional as well as local scale.

The Designer as Symbol Maker

The modern industrial designer decorates everyday consumer goods with symbols in order to express the aspirations of today's culture. This role overrides the designer's other roles: salesman, packager, consumer's representative.

There is a direct ratio between the importance of the modern artifact and the extent to which it is decorated. Scientific instruments—the surgeon's scalpel, the astronomer's telescope, the chemist's flask—lack ornament and are, therefore, appreciated as sculpture by those who share the contemporary

Russel Wright. American Modern dinnerware, Steubenville Pottery Co., Rome, N. Y. 1937

Eva Zeisel. Museum White dinnerware, Castleton China, New Castle, Pa. 1946

Raymond Loewy Associates. Model SX-42, Hallicrafters Communications Receiver, Chicago. 1946

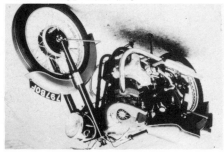

Staff design. BSA motorcycle, Birmingham, England. Introduced 1955; later model shown

Willys Motors and Army Ordnance staff design. Jeep. Willys Motors, Toledo, Ohio. Introduced 1941; later model shown

A. P. Oakley & Co. Raleigh bicycle, England. Introduced 1925; 1957 model shown

F. Porsche. Porsche 1500 Super. Stuttgart, 1952

Raymond Loewy Associates. Studebaker Starlight, Studebaker Corporation, U.S.A. 1947

John Thornley. MG model TC, MG Car Co., Abingdon-on-Thames, England. 1945

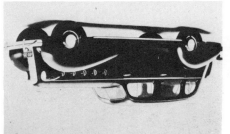

Staff design. LaSalle, General Motors, Detroit, 1935

Staff design. Rolls-Royce Phantom II, Crewe, England. 1930

1 Henry Ford, Edsel Ford and Joseph Galamb. Ford Model T, U.S.A. 1923

Gordon Buehrig. Cord 810. U.S.A. 1936.

Staff design. Volkswagen, Germany. 1936

Edsel Ford and E. T. Gregorie.
Lincoln Continental, Dearborn. 1941

G. Bertone. Citroen, DS—19, Citroen,
Paris. 1955

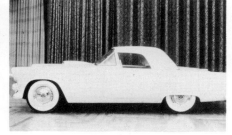

George Walker, Robert Maguire, Elwood Engel.
Thunderbird, Ford Motor Company,
Dearborn. 1956.

Staff design. VW-Karmann-Ghia,
Germany. 1959

General Motors staff and
Raymond Loewy Associates.
Greyhound Scenicruiser bus,
Pontiac, Mich. 1954

Staff design. Douglas DC–3,
Douglas Aircraft Co., Santa Monica, Calif. 1935

Staff design. Budd Pioneer Zephyr.
Budd Company, U.S.A. 1934

Carl Otto. Edison Voicewriter dictating machine, U.S.A. 1952

Staff design. Hermes Rocket Portable typewriter, Europe. 1932

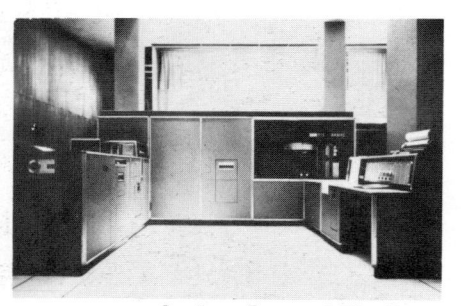

Sundberg–Ferar and Eliot Noyes. IBM 305 Ramac computer, U.S.A. 1955

preference for form over pattern. Paradoxically, absence of ornament conveys a message: that modern life is dominated by machinery. By eschewing ornament, a Braun Company radio, for example, is made to imitate the unornamented milling and stamping machines with which it was made. Because consumer goods—TV sets, vacuum cleaners and outboard motors—are purchased for their symbolic significance as well as their usefulness, they are usually highly sculpted.

The Iconography of the Automobile

The decrease in the usefulness of the automobile may be measured by the increasing irrationality of its form and the increasing number of escutcheons and iconographic devices that decorate it. This iconography clusters around symbols of prestige and power. Among over 350 models on the American market in the late 1960's were dozens with names of weapons including American Motors' Javelin, Ford's Cutlass, Buick LeSabre and Dodge Dart. Others named models after aggressive animals: Cougar, Mustang, Charger, Wildcat, Barracuda. And still others named models for violent states of weather, including the General Motors Tempest and Cyclone.

Fashion: The Shorthand of Style

Mod has made fashionable the earlier look of the 1930's. Twiggy's Vidal Sassoon haircut recapitulated Betty Boop's bob. The subject of Roy Lichtenstein's *Big Painting* (page 111) is the brush stroke technique of Abstract Expressionism. His dot rendering technique transforms the dots of the Ives halftone process into decoration. Thus fashion reiterates the looks of preceding generations. The current generation, scanning, classifying and absorbing earlier models, articulates a new look expressive of its unique life experience.

Fashion in consumer goods of the 1910–1940 period was dictated by the innovations of prior decades. Rietveld translated Mondrian's paintings into the Schroeder House. American industrial designers then translated the Schroeder House into thousands of consumer products. The streamlined Scotch-tape dispensers of the 1940's imitated the tapered aircraft of the 1930's. The blunt-nosed electric irons of the 1950's imitated the diesel locomotives of the 1930's, and the tail-finned autos of the 1950's imitated the finned missiles of late World War II. By extension, sport is to physical activity what fashion is to style. Instead of recapitulating style, sport recapitulates technology. Sailing became a sport when steam replaced sail. When gunpowder made the longbows that won the day at Agincourt obsolete, archery became a sport.

Gifford Jackson (overleaf), in *Industrial Design,* September 1962, charted five successive fashions in American product design since 1920. Jackson's "Stepform," the hard-edge fashion of the 1920's, corresponds to Functionalist product design, while "Streamform," the soft-edge fashion of the same period, corresponds to Expressionist product design. "Taperform" and "Sheerform" retranslate both stylistic modes into alternate soft and hard fashions for the 1950's. For the 1960's Jackson predicted "Facetform" and "Sculptureform," a further permutation of Functionalist and Expressionist product design.

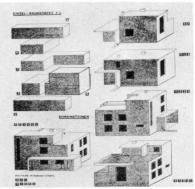

Walter Gropius.
Project for standardized serial houses, Bauhaus, Germany. 1921

Konrad Wachsmann.
Structural system for shelter, U.S.A. 1953

Moshe Safdie. Habitat apartments, Expo '67, Montreal. 1967

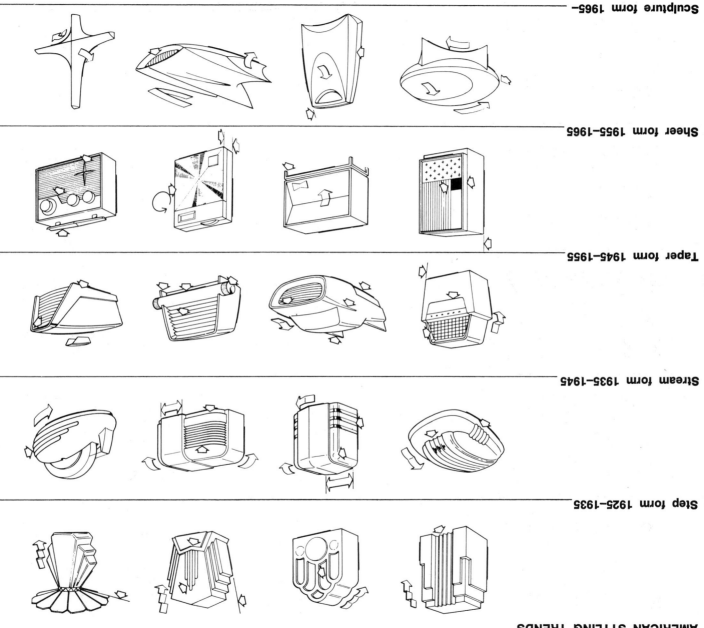

Sculpture form 1965–

Sheer form 1955–1965

Taper form 1945–1955

Stream form 1935–1945

Step form 1925–1935

AMERICAN STYLING TRENDS

Gifford Jackson. Trends in styling of industrially designed products, U.S.A. 1962

Oskar Kokoschka. *The Tragedy of Man,* Germany. 1908

Fillippo Tommaso Marinetti. *Parole in Liberta,* Italy. 1912–1914

El Lissitzky. *Merz* program cover, Germany, n.d.

MODERN GRAPHIC DESIGN

Kokoschka, Kirchner and other members of *Die Breucke* and *Der Blaue Reiter,* the original Expressionist movements, established a tradition of Expressionist graphic design in the first dozen years of the 20th century. In this tradition designers manipulated layouts to enhance their emotional intensity. It was carried forward in the Dadaist magazine, *Merz* (1923–1932), in which designers placed type in a seemingly irrational way for startling effect. Kurt Schwitters and Hans Richter, who inserted type as a decorative device in Dadaist collages, also advanced Expressionist graphics. To a lesser degree, Surrealism, in which the juxtaposition of seemingly unrelated objects is used to suggest the irrationality of the unconscious mind, influenced poster design from the late 1930's until the early 1950's.

The Expressionists handled color impulsively and exaggerated forms to heighten emotion. They were preoccupied with anxiety, death, sex and other highly charged subjects. Abstraction, when it appeared, for example, in the paintings of Kandinsky, was lyrical and expressive rather than analytical and rational. Expressionists made woodcuts and explored other handcrafts rather than applying modern techniques.

The Expressionist painters and graphic designers were stirred by new discoveries in psychology and biology. Sigmund Freud, in a series of psychoanalytic publications that began in 1895 with an investigation of dreams, revealed the child that lives in the adult, the primitive savage behind the civilized mask. Freud suggested that the difference between the sane and the insane is quantitative rather than qualitative.

Expressionist painters converted these unsettling ideas into paintings permeated with the childlike, the primitive and the irrational. Darwin's theory of evolution provided turn-of-the-century scholars a model for translating history into biological metaphors. It also stimulated the interest of 20th-century designers in nature-derived forms. Wright's "organic" architecture, in which the house appeared to grow out of its site, established an Expressionist tradition that continues today. The Bertoia chair (page 88) and the Harper light (page 91) both consist of an indeterminate number of components and thus imply the possibility of growth.

Although Futurists held different views from the Expressionists, their "free typography" was Expressionist in intent and appearance. Growing out of Marinetti's "free-word" poetry, in which meaning was determined by special relationships between words rather than by conventional syntax, "free typography" was introduced in the pages of the Futurist periodical, *Lacerba* (1913–1914). It destroyed the conventional symmetry of the printed page as it had been laid out since the invention of movable type. The editors of *Lacerba,*

Giovanni Papini and Ardengo Soffici, placed type according to emphasis and let pictures and headlines fall at random. They ignored the conventions of using similar type faces on the same page and of placing printing so that it could run only from left to right.

Cubism, de Stijl and Constructivism

The Expressionists were exponents of freedom; the Cubists encouraged order, geometric regularity and abstraction in graphic design. Even Cubist interest in the primitive art of Africa was due to the discovery—by Picasso and others —of the evocative power of abstraction. Between 1909 and 1912 this led to Analytical Cubism, in which artists eliminated conventional subject matter in favor of abstract, geometric compositions.

The Cubists also incorporated into paintings and posters the lesson taught by Einstein's Theory of Relativity, promulgated in 1905. This theory killed conventional perspective insofar as it suggested to artists that they need not view the world from a fixed point. Picasso, for example, in *Les Demoiselles D'Avignon,* used a new cinematic perspective to show figures from all sides at once. He converted the models themselves into scarcely human abstract volumes.

The French artist and architect Le Corbusier developed a kind of Cubistic painting style called Purism, in which he worked with the geometric forms Cézanne had described. His early buildings, particularly the Villa Savoye (page 81), are essentially Cubist sculpture. Other designers also echoed the Cubist predilection for geometric forms. Loos had introduced them in the Steiner house (page 75), Wright in chairs (page 87) and Behrens in teakettles (page 56) and other electric appliances even before 1910. Cassandre and Léger, among others, soon produced posters with a Cubist flavor.

Two extensions of Cubism—de Stijl and Constructivism—were the primary influence on Functionalist typography and poster design.

Fundamental elements in de Stijl graphic design were asymmetrical but rational disposition of type, rectilinear patterns, and red, yellow, blue, black and white color schemes. The Stijl group, formed in Leyden in 1917, issued its first manifesto the following year. This manifesto promised to "abolish natural form." The painters Piet Mondrian and Theo van Doesburg and the architects Gerrit Rietveld and J. J. P. Oud experimented with type and lay-out in the magazine de *Stijl,* which they began to publish in October, 1917.

In 1920 van Doesburg met Mies, Gropius, Mendelsohn and Le Corbusier, and in 1922 he began to visit the Bauhaus. Many Bauhaus publications show the influence of de Stijl. Universal, the type face designed by the director of

Herbert Bayer. Universal type face, Bauhaus, Germany. 1925

Eric Gill. Gill sans serif, England. 1928

Paul Renner. Futura type face, Germany. 1927

Staff design. Burroughs Corporation. E13B. The fourteen characters in magnetically read alphabet, U.S.A. 1958

Robert Reed and Tom Daly, U.S.A. 1967

das freundliche Handzeichen

Hans Muller-Brockman, Switzerland, 1950

Olivetti Studio 44

Staff design, Olivetti, Italy, 1944

Ludwig Hohlwein, Germany, c. 1935

I WANT YOU FOR U.S.ARMY
NEAREST RECRUITING STATION

James Flagg, U.S.A. c. 1918

J. S. Leyendecker, U.S.A. c. 1910

Aldo Mazza, Italy, 1910

McKnight Kauffer. England. 1929

Jan Tschichold. Germany. c. 1924

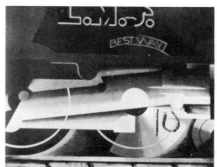

Cassandre. France. c. 1920

Robert Bereny. Italy. c. 1930

Henri Matisse. France. 1947

Fernand Léger. France. c. 1948

Milton Glaser. U.S.A. 1968

Roy Lichtenstein. U.S.A. 1967

Robert Rauschenberg. U.S.A. 1970

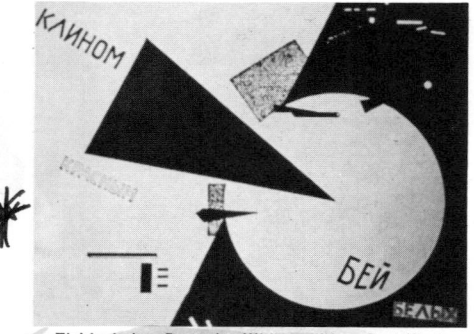

El Lissitzky. *Beat the Whites with a Red Wedge,* U.S.S.R. 1919

Anonymous. Communist political poster, Russia. 1930

Anonymous. Nazi political poster, Germany. c. 1928–1938

the Bauhaus typography shop, Herbert Bayer, achieves a simplicity of form appropriate to de Stijl layout. Bayer employed only lower-case letters in the belief that upper-case letters were unnecessary and that the German practice of capitalizing every noun in a sentence decreased legibility. After World War I Eric Gill introduced Gill Sans Serif and Paul Renner Futura, both faces without serifs.

Max Bill extended both the Futurist experiments in random placement and the de Stijl practice of asymmetrical layout with flush-left and ragged-right type boxes, interspersed with dramatic areas of white space. Refinements on de Stijl and Futurist practices also were made by Joost Schmidt at the Bauhaus, and later by Leipzig-born Jan Tschichold. Tschichold consolidated the findings of de Stijl and Bauhaus innovators in *Die Neue Typographie* (1928) and in *Eine Stunde Druckgestaltung* (1931), a major work on modern graphics translated by the Czech-born designer Ladislav Sutnar and reprinted in 1959 in *Typography U.S.A.*

Computer typography differs in principle as well as look from any that has existed previously. A computer type face is, in effect, a series of physical symbols to be read optically by humans and magnetically by machines. In order for a computer to read a given symbol, it must be printed in magnetic ink and broken up into areas that give a positive or negative electric signal depending on whether the amount of ink in that area is sufficient to register. The computer's electronic reading head does not read the character as a shape but section by section on a finely controlled time basis. In the face shown here, E13B, each number is divided into seventy blocks or sensing areas and printed in magnetic ink. An electronic register records the presence or absence of magnetic ink in each of these sensing areas and thus builds up an image of the printed character. The American Bankers Association developed E13B in cooperation with computer equipment manufacturers, and today it is used by many American and British banks for the automatic reading and sorting of bank checks.

The Abstract Poster

De Stijl and Constructivist designers invented for the abstract poster a new graphic vocabulary of column rules, type and geometric blocks of color. The Russian Constructivist El Lissitzky (1890–1941) designed the first abstract poster, "Beat the Whites with the Red Wedge." In it Constructivist geometry prevails. The negative boundary equals the positive boundary, the wedge is a perfect triangle and the circle perfect. Since negative and positive space are equal, only the dynamic leaning axis creates tension. Although an early effort at Communist propaganda, the design overshadows the message by breaking words apart and scattering them.

Perhaps Lissitzky realized that abstraction was more appropriate to his Prouns, or abstract paintings, than to posters, whose purpose is immediate and powerful communication. In any event he pioneered photomontage as a poster device. Reconfirming the power of the concrete image, photomontage became the most important single new element in 20th-century poster design.

Herbert Matter (1907–   ), who studied under Léger and the French poster designer Cassandre, popularized the photomontage poster in a mid-1930's campaign for the Swiss National Tourist Office. Matter commands attention by juxtaposing large- and small-scale objects unexpectedly and by presenting type in free, unconventional positions. Josef Muller-Brockmann (1914–   ), stage-set and exhibit designer and co-editor of *Neue Grafik,* is another Swiss master of the photomontage poster.

Prior to and during World War II, German designers exploited the power of the photographic image in posters consisting of the name and face of Adolf Hitler. Hitler had noted in *Mein Kampf* (1925) the importance of the poster in marshalling public sentiment. Despite the trend toward photo-montage posters, the German designer Ludwig Hohlwein continued to work with the drawn image when he turned to designing posters for the Nazi party in the 1930's. Important post-war German graphic designers include O. H. W. Hadank (trademarks), George Grosz (drawings), Otl Aicher (posters, typography and packaging) and Hermann Zapf (typography).

In America during the interwar years W. A. Dwiggins, Bruce Rogers, Daniel Updike and Frederic Goudy preserved a clean typographic classicism as exemplified in books published by Alfred Knopf. Working as graphic designers rather than typographers, Alvin Lustig, William Golden, Paul Rand, Lester Beall, Rudolph de Harak, Saul Bass and Ivan Chermayeff were among the important American designers of the post-World War II years. In addition Bauhaus-educated Gyorgy Kepes, who is now teaching at MIT, introduced the visual landscape of science to graphic designers after World War II. German-born Will Burtin (1908–   ) emphasized science as a new dimension in art and interpreted complex information on the brain, the atom and the cell in animated three-dimensional models. Swiss-born Erik Nitsche (1908–   ) refocused the image of General Dynamics Corporation from that of major American weapons-maker to that of peace-maker in an Atoms for Peace poster campaign of 1965.

Herbert Matter. Swiss Tourist Office poster, Switzerland. 1936

Josef Albers.
Exercise for Fundamental Design Course, Bauhaus, Germany. 1926

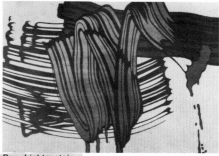

Roy Lichtenstein.
U.S.A. 1967

THE ELECTRIC CIRCUS

Op and Pop

Two contemporary branches of painting, Op and Pop, while maintaining Functionalist and Expressionist traditions, had a distinct influence on contemporary American graphic design. The Op tradition, which goes back to Josef Albers' experiments at the Bauhaus, has been reaffirmed since the mid-1960's in the work of Saul Bass.

The Pop Art preoccupation with life in the 1930's, while Expressionist in its nostalgia, parallels the preoccupation of the pre-Raphaelite painters with life in the Middle Ages. Pop attests to the social significance of the depiction of trivia by serious artists. Pop's emphasis on subject matter over technique parallels an earlier similar emphasis in the work of members of *Die Breucke* and *Der Blaue Reiter.* Andy Warhol's Brillo boxes and soup cans comment on the vulgarity of commercial graphic design, and sophisticated commercial graphic design has turned to self-parody as a device in sales promotion.

Modern Trademarks

Even small-scale industries and corporations today have learned to entrust the design of their trademarks to a professional graphic designer. Therefore, contemporary trademarks are vastly more sophisticated than those of the Victorian period. Precisely because they are designed by art-school-trained professionals, they closely reflect trends in the realm of painting. When painting flew to abstraction after World War II, trademarks rapidly followed suit. Those shown here, though individually handsome, look similar because each designer strove for a similar abstract effect.

Ivan Chermayeff. Mark for discotheque, *U.S.A. c. 1968*

Lester Beall. International Paper Company,
U.S.A. c. 1958

William Golden. CBS, U.S.A. c. 1955

Herbert Matter. New Haven Rairoad,
U.S.A. c. 1955

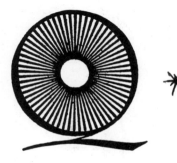

Paul Rand.
International Business Machines, U.S.A.
1957

Gottlieb Daimler. Mercedes–Benz,
Germany. Original mark c. 1900;
mark in present form since 1923

F. H. Ehmcke.
Mark for a photographer,
Germany. c. 1960

Anonymous. London Transport,
London. c. 1914

Gerald Holton.
Campaign for Nuclear Disarmament,
London. c. 1960

Ernst Keller.
Mark for tailor, Germany. c. 1960

MODERN PHOTOGRAPHY

Alfred Stieglitz (1864–1964) saw photography as a unique medium. He expanded the realm of photography by shooting rain, snow and twilight—conditions previously considered impossible to capture. Born in Hoboken of German-immigrant parents, Stieglitz studied engineering and photography at the Berlin Polytechnic Institute from 1882 to 1890. He worked for a photo-engraving firm on returning to New York and began taking street-life photos of the city with a hand-held camera.

Influenced by Emerson, Stieglitz organized the Photo-Secession group in 1902. The group aimed to secede from art photography as it was then practiced. But many members continued to produce soft-lined photos of romantic subjects. Stieglitz alone practiced "straight" photography. He used line, form and shadow to achieve the same emotional impact as painting. To demonstrate photography as an art, Steiglitz hung photographs by Paul Strand, Alvin Coburn and Edward Steichen next to paintings by Matisse, Picasso and Cezanne at 291, the Fifth Avenue gallery he operated from 1905 to 1917. During the same years Stieglitz published the influential photography magazine *Camera Work*. Having proved to his own satisfaction that photography was an art, albeit produced by a machine, Stieglitz said, "It has been done—the machine has plastically expressed life—a mechanically printed piece of paper breathes—it is a concrete thing—itself—different from anything else in the world. And yet it is the human controlling it—leading it—to breathe his vision, through the mechanism, into the final concrete object—the photograph."

The New Vision

Cubism, Constructivism and de Stijl had opened a new landscape of abstract pattern and pure form. They inspired photographers to create abstract photos. Through montage, collage, solarization and other manipulative techniques, photographers began to break up and distort the conventional photographic image. Boston-born Alvin Langdon Coburn (1882–1966), influenced by the Cubist painter Max Weber, was the first to exploit the fact that the camera could create abstract pattern as well as capture real images. Although his early portraits and street scenes were in an evocative soft-focus vein, he turned in 1917 to the Vortograph, an abstract photo whose name was derived from Ezra Pound's Vorticist band of rebel poets and painters. Coburn produced Vortographs with multiple exposures on the same plate, prisms that split the image into segments and lenses placed inside a triangle of mirrors. The German Dadaist painter Christian Schad followed Coburn's experiments

Alfred Stieglitz. *The Terminal,* U.S.A. 1893

Alfred Stieglitz. *The Steerage,* U.S.A. 1907

A. L. Coburn. *Pillars of Smoke, Pittsburgh.* 1910

a year later with the Schadograph. This looked like a Cubist collage and was made by placing cut-outs on sensitized paper.

Man Ray (1890–   ), originally a painter and maker of Dadaist collages and constructions, turned to abstract photography after World War I. He rediscovered the process of solarization in 1926. Known since 1862 as the Sabattier effect, solarization partially reverses the negative into a positive image by a short exposure to light. Ray used this technique to make semi-abstract and abstract photographs. He also experimented with camera-less photos, which he made by projecting the shadows of three-dimensional objects onto sensitized paper. The Dadaist poet Tristian Tzara published a series of these photos, called Rayographs, in *Champs Delicieux* (1922).

A. L. Coburn. *Vortograph,* U.S.A. 1917

At the Bauhaus Laszlo Moholy-Nagy explored the relationship between painting, photography and films. Unlike Emerson and Stieglitz, Moholy-Nagy saw nothing wrong with altering film and manipulating the print during development. His fidelity was not to nature as seen by the human eye but to a Platonic world of perfect abstract patterns. To create such patterns he experimented with reticulation, or the breaking-up of emulsion by application of heat; photograms, or abstract photos created without a camera; and photomontage —the superimposing of part of one photo on another.

Moholy-Nagy aroused interest in aerial photos and photos taken from unusual angles because of their ability to reveal patterns theretofore unnoticed. He also deliberately distorted and exaggerated images to emphasize their inherent design. The typephoto, a photo on which type has been printed, was Moholy-Nagy's most important contribution to graphic design. Herbert Matter, Herbert Bayer, Jan Tschichold and El Lissitzky brilliantly translated Moholy's idea into the photographic poster.

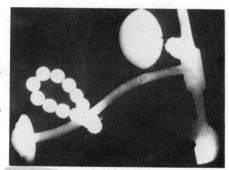

Man Ray. *Rayograph,* U.S.A. 1929

The New Manipulators

Harry Callahan (1918–   ) and Ray Metzker (1931–   ) are more recent photographers who manipulate film, lens or printing process to achieve highly designed effects. Callahan, the third-generation leader of the art-in-photography movement, converts weeds, leaves and other elements from the natural landscape into exotic abstractions by isolating them from their environment. The Surrealist effect of *Eleanor,* in which one negative is superimposed on another, was achieved by the juxtaposition of unrelated subject matter and a reversal of normal scale—the figure of Eleanor tiny in relation to the tree-sized twigs of the background underbrush. Surrealist photographs have also been made by the British photographers Cecil Beaton (1906–   ) and Bill Brandt (1905–   ). With *Les Enfants Terribles,* the French poet Jean

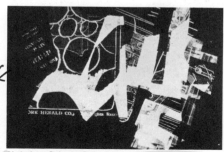

Christian Schad. *Schadograph,* Germany. 1918

Cocteau popularized the Surrealist film.

Aaron Siskind's (1903–   ) photographs transform walls, pavements and other elements in the urban landscape into abstract compositions. Sharp edge, extreme contrast and flattening out of planes distinguish Siskind's photos. Unlike Ray Metzker and others, he does not manipulate film or print. Of Siskind's photographs the art critic Harold Rosenberg has said, "Instead of scenes that seem like paintings, Siskind's pictures are paintings as they appear on the printed page—which is where most people today see most of the paintings that they see. They are reproductions that have no originals."

The Photographer as Diarist of Nature

Siskind and Callahan turned to natural subjects in order to abstract their patterns. But Edward Weston, Ansel Adams and Minor White select natural subjects in order to record their intrinsic beauty. Concerned with maximum control of light, film and printing, and committed to their craft with priestlike devotion, they make pictorial diaries resembling the notebooks of a naturalist. In the tradition of William Henry Jackson, Edward Weston (1886–1958) photographed the natural splendors of the American West. He called attention to "the unique quality of photography to record continuous tone." *California and the West* (1940) and *My Camera on Point Lobos* (1950) make his vision of nature permanent. These books included studies of green peppers and snail shells, as well as startling close-ups of the human face.

Working in the tradition of Weston, Ansel Adams (1902–   ) has brought home the glories of the Yosemite and beyond in *The High Sierra* (1927) and *This is the American Earth* (1964). After a first visit to Yosemite in 1927, "a momentous experience—so intense as to be almost painful," he returned annually for photographic pilgrimages.

Minor White (1908–   ) defines the photograph as a mirage and the camera as a metamorphizing machine. In his search to "free himself of the tyranny of the visual fact," he transforms a single rock into a vast landscape, a frosted window pane into a sea wave.

Photo-journalism

The London Illustrated Weekly began to publish photographs after the invention of the halftone process in 1874, but not until Henry Luce founded *Life* in 1937 did photo-journalism come into its own. Margaret Bourke-White (1905–   ), prototype of the photo-journalist, did the first cover for *Life* and

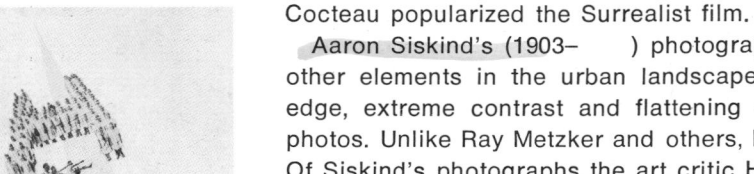

Laszlo Moholy–Nagy. *Photomontage,* Germany. c. 1925

Harry Callahan. *Eleanor,* U.S.A. 1951

Ray Metzker. *Composition,* U.S.A. 1965–1966

wrote about, as well as photographed, General Patton's crossing of the Rhine in World War II, the North African invasion and the war in Korea. The picture story as it is known today was partly shaped by Alfred Eisenstaedt (1898–   ), David Douglas Duncan (1916–   ) and Eugene Smith (1918–   ). A highly suggestive genre of communication, the picture story arranges theme-related photos and text for maximum impact.

The New Realists

The 35-mm Leica, introduced in 1924, brought a new realism to photography. Ease of carrying, relative unobtrusiveness and remarkably fast shutter speeds (even in early models up to $\frac{1}{1000}$ of a second) made it possible to capture faster action with less light than ever before. In the fleeting instant, humble and great alike were caught off-guard. Action at the edge of the frame, characteristic of the 35-mm photo, implied that each photo had been sliced from the living tissue of a moment and that life continued immediately beyond the edge of each frame. These characteristics balanced the 35-mm photograph in a perfect equation with reality.

Aaron Siskind. *Harlan, Kentucky,* U.S.A. 1951

Eric Salomon (1886–1944), son of a Berlin banker of failing fortune, began working in the publicity department of a German movie firm. He bought his first camera, the tiny Ermanox, simply as a tool for his work. Later he became a full-time photographer. Often concealing his camera with great imagination, he photographed forbidden court hearings, important diplomatic conferences and inaccessible social gatherings. An incorruptible but compassionate photographer, Salomon photographed Aristide Briand and Raymond Poincaré at the League of Nations; Communists and Nazis at the Reichstag; Gigli, Toscanini and Yehudi Menuhin in the midst of performances; William Randolph Hearst and Marion Davies in the midst of dinner. *Graphic,* the London magazine, coined the phrase "candid camera" for his work.

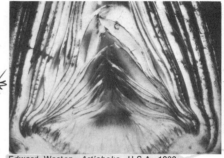

Edward Weston. *Artichoke,* U.S.A. 1930

Salomon thought of himself as a visual recorder of history. While he had the foresight to save his negatives from the Nazis by burying one set behind the chicken-coop of a Dutch farm and depositing a second set in the library of the Dutch Parliament, he did not save himself. Salomon and his wife and one son were gassed at Auschwitz in 1944.

Henri Cartier-Bresson (1908–   ), the master of the "decisive moment," concerns himself with revealing an equally true but different aspect of life. He communicates his own vision to the viewer by capturing the moment when emotion and action are in greatest tension.

In the United States the Farm Security Agency offered Dorothea Lange (1895–1966) and Walker Evans an opportunity to record the pathos of De-

Ansel Adams. *Gates of the Valley,* Yosemite, Calif. 1936

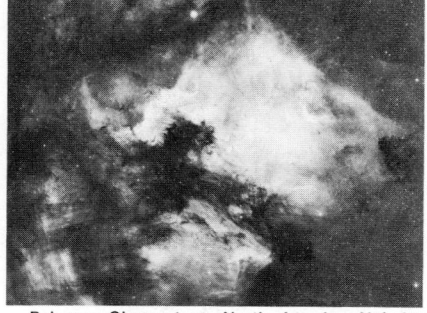

Palomar Observatory. North America Nebula, U.S.A. 1968

pression America. *Let Us Now Praise Famous Men* combined Evans's photos with James Agee's account of Southern sharecroppers. Lange's visual report on the plight of the dust bowl farmers moved John Steinbeck to write *Grapes of Wrath* (1937). Her photo of a white overseer comments tellingly on race relations. Diane Arbus, Robert Frank, William Gedney, Danny Lyon and Bruce Davidson, the apparently objective but actually critical documenters of the current American scene, continue to use photography as a weapon of social and political comment.

Once-Invisible Worlds

As early as 1911 Wilson's cloud chamber made it possible to photograph the atom. Since that time a powerful and undeniable—but elusive—parallel has been revealed between the patterns of the scientific photograph and the patterns of abstract painting. The electron micrograph, the *schlieren* photograph, the infrared and ultraviolet photograph and the strobe photograph have revealed the geometric perfection of worlds too far away, too small or too fast to be seen by the unaided human eye. They have expanded the visual imagination of a generation and have resolved the apparent conflict between the biomorphic and geometric traditions of form. The object biomorphically irregular to the naked eye discloses its perfect geometry when observed and photographed by electron microscope.

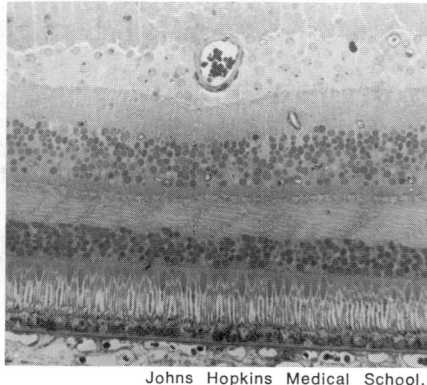

Johns Hopkins Medical School.
Human retina magnified 175 times, U.S.A. 1965

Crew of Apollo 11.
Earth taken from moon, U.S.A. 1969

Eric Salomon. *Banquet at Quai d'Orsay*, Germany. c. 1935

Diane Arbus. Untitled, U.S.A. c. 1962

William Gedney. *Girls in Appalachia*, U.S.A. 1966

Henri Cartier–Bresson. *Picnic on Banks of Marne*, France. 1938

Bruce Davidson. *Trapper and Wife*, U.S.A. 1966

Danny Lyon. *Uptown Chicago*, U.S.A. 1965

Dorothea Lange. *Plantation Overseer and His Field Hands*, Mississippi. 1936

Robert Frank. *Hoboken*, U.S.A. 1955

George Krause. *Qui Reposa?*, U.S.A. 1967

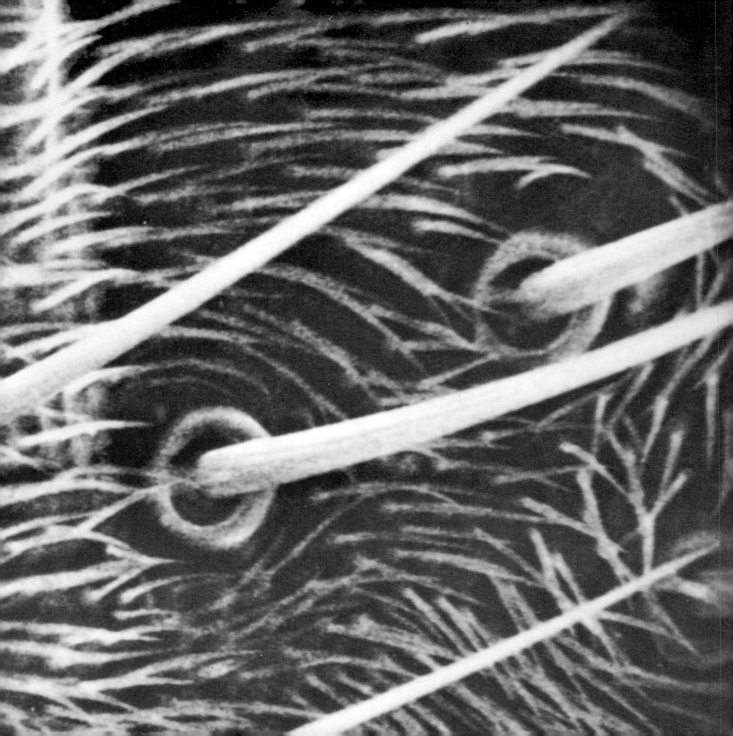

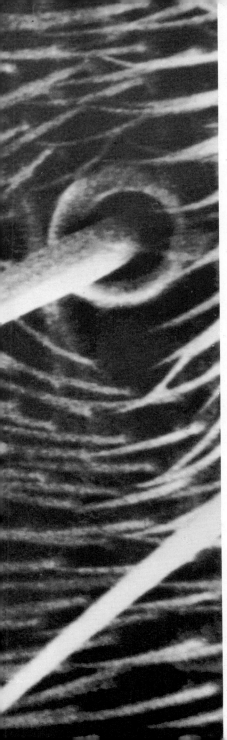

PHOTO CREDITS

Numbers refer to pages in the text. The letters
a to *c* designate top, middle, and bottom
positions on each page, except on pages
where there are more than three illustrations.
On such pages the letters *a* to *i* designate
left, center, and right photographs running
across top of page, then middle of page,
then bottom of page.

6, George Eastman House
8*a*, Hamilton Watch Company
10*a*, Metropolitan Museum of Art; 8*c*, National
   Gallery of Art
12–13, Gernsheim Collection
15*a, b, c*, British Travel Association
16*b, c*, French Government Tourist Office
17*c*, French Government Tourist Office
18*a*, Gary Haycock; 18*c*, Smithsonian
   Institution
19*a*, Pam Service; 19*c*, Herbert Solomon
20*a*, Preservation Society of Newport County
21*a*, Wayne Andrews; 21*b*. Preservation Society
   of Newport County; 21*c*, Frederica Leser
24*a*, Seymour Lipitz
28*a*, Morris Gallery; 28*b*, Gerd Hatje; 28*c*,
   Morris Gallery
30*a*, Brooklyn Museum; 30*b*, Preservation
   Society of Newport County; 30*c*, Gary Haycock
31*a*, Brooklyn Museum; 31*b*, Gary Haycock
38*a–i*, AT&T Photo Service
46*a*, N.Y. Public Library; 46*b*, Gernsheim
   Collection
47*c*, Gernsheim Collection
48*a*, Gernsheim Collection; 48*b*, c, George
   Eastman House
49*a*, George Eastman House; 49*b*, c, Gernsheim
   Collection
50*a*, Metropolitan Museum of Art; 50*b, c,*
   Gernsheim Collection; 50*d*, Metropolitan
   Museum uf Art; 50*e*, Gernsheim Collection;
   50*h*, McGill University, Notman Photographic
   Archives; 50*i*, Gernsheim Collection
51*a*, Gernsheim Collection; 51*c*, George Eastman
   House
52*a*, George Eastman House; 52*b*, McGill
   University, Notman Photographic Archives
54–55, John Szarkowski (from *The Idea of
   Louis Sullivan*, U. of Ill. Press)
56*a*, Bally Museum of Shoes
57*b*, Photo Mas, Barcelona
59*b*, Kingspor Museum, Offenbach
62*a, c*, Gernsheim Collection; 62*d, e*, George
   Eastman House; 62*f*, George Bohot; 62*g*,
   Gernsheim Collection; 62*i*, Deutsche
   Fotothek, Dresden
63*a, b, c*, George Eastman House
65*a*, Landesgewerbeamt, Baden–Württemburg
66*b, c*, Landesgewerbeamt, Baden–Württemburg
67*a*, Landesgewerbeamt, Baden–Württemburg
68*d*, Glasgow University Art Collections
70*a, b*, Gerd Hatje; 70*c*, Glasgow University
   School of Art
71*a, b*, Gerd Hatje

Closeup of the eyebrow of a fly,
magnified about 700 times.

74*a*, Herbert Solomon; 74*b*, Photo Chevon
75*b*, Gerd Hatje
80*a*, Gemeente Musea van Amsterdam
84*c*, William Teitlebaum
86*a, b*, Museum of Modern Art
87*b*, Gemeente Musea van Amsterdam
88*c, d*, Contemporary Arts Museum; 88*i*, Knoll
   Associates
89*c*, Atelier, International; 89*d*, Alexandre
   Georges; 89*e*, Knoll Associates; 89*g*, Alexandre
   Georges; 89*h*; Michael Schachner
91*c*, Richard Klenk
93*c*, Norm Ulrich Studio
95*a*, William C. Dobie
97*a, b*, courtesy Jay Doblin
98*a, b, c*, courtesy Jay Doblin
99*a, b, c*, courtesy Jay Doblin
100–101, all photographs courtesy Jay Doblin
102, all photographs courtesy Jay Doblin
104–105, chart courtesy Gifford Jackson
114*a, b*, Gernsheim Collection
119*a, d*, Gernsheim Collection
120, National Aeronautics and Space
   Administration
124, National Aeronautics and Space
   Administration
Jacket front, Danny Lyon, Magnum
Jacket back, Gernsheim Collection

Acknowledgments

This book is largely the outgrowth of a course in the history of modern design taught by the author at Pratt Institute, 1965-1969, and at Parsons School of Design, 1968-1969. Many students were helpful both in supplying research and photographs. Ethel Strainchamps and John Berseth contributed to the editorial process. Suzanne Clarke and Chaim Shatan provided personal encouragement.

Geodesic construction, Drop City, Colorado. 1967

INDEX

Astronaut floats into space during
Gemini-Titan 4 flight. 1965